Amelia Earhart

PIONEERING AVIATOR AND
FORCE FOR WOMEN'S RIGHTS

By Diane Dakers

Crabtree Publishing Company
www.crabtreebooks.com

Crabtree Publishing Company
www.crabtreebooks.com

Author: Diane Dakers
Publishing plan research and development:
Reagan Miller
Project coordinator: Mark Sachner,
Editors: Mark Sachner, Lynn Peppas
Proofreader: Kathy Middleton
Indexer: Gini Holland
Editorial director: Kathy Middleton
Photo research: Ruth Owen
Designer: Westgraphix/Tammy West
Proofreader: Petrice Custance
Production: Kim Richardson
Prepress technician: Ken Wright
Print Coordinator: Kathy Berti

Produced by Water Buffalo Books

Photographs and reproductions:
Alamy: © Trinity Mirror/Mirrorpix: pp. 7 (top), 57 (bottom); © AF Archive: p. 15; © B. Christopher: p. 21; © Paul Briden: p. 45; © Glasshouse Images: p. 61; © PF-(aircraft): p. 80; © Everett Collection: p. 81; © PF-(sdasm2): p. 83 (bottom); © John Frost Newspapers: p. 94; © Tribune Content Agency LLC: p. 98; © Moviestore collection Ltd.: p. 100; © Pictorial Press Ltd: p. 103; **Corbis:** © Yann Arthus-Bertrand/Corbis: p. 76; **Jeff Dakers:** pp. 40–41; **European Space Agency:** p. 9 (center right); **Flickr:** © Tekniska museet: p. 54; **Tony Frost:** p. 59; **Getty Images:** © New York Times Co.: p. 20 (center); **Granger:** © Granger, NYC: cover (background); **NASA:** p. 9 (bottom left); **Public domain:** pp. 7 (bottom), 12 (center), 12 (bottom), 13 (top), 13 (center), 33, 35, 38 (top), 47, 57 (top), 64 (bottom), 76, 79, 85; **Shutterstock:** © Everett Collection: pp. 4 (top), 11, 23, 29, 32 (top), 32 (bottom), 43 (bottom), 63 (bottom), 64 (top), 68 (top), 71, 73, 83 (top), 87, 91, 93 (bottom); © Emka74: p. 12 (top); © catwalker: p. 16; p. 41 (top); © Anton Ivanov: p. 99; © Neftali: p. 101; **Wikipedia/Creative Commons:** cover (foreground), pp. 1, 4 (bottom), 5, 8 (top), 8 (bottom), 9 (top right), 9 (top left), 9 (bottom right), 13 (bottom), 17, 19 (top), 19 (bottom), 20 (top), 25, 35 (top), 37, 38 (bottom), 39, 49, 50, 52, 63 (top), 67, 68 (bottom), 69, 72, 75 (top), 75 (bottom), 90, 93 (top), 102.

Publisher's note:
All quotations in this book come from original sources and contain the spelling and grammatical inconsistencies of the original text. Some of the quotations may also contain terms that are no longer in use and may be considered inappropriate or offensive. The use of such terms is for the sake of preserving the historical and literary accuracy of the sources and should not be seen as encouraging or endorsing the use of such terms today.

Library and Archives Canada Cataloguing in Publication

Dakers, Diane, author
        Amelia Earhart : pioneering aviator and force for women's rights / Diane Dakers.

(Crabtree groundbreaker biographies)
Includes index.
Issued in print and electronic formats.
ISBN 978-0-7787-2562-6 (bound).--ISBN 978-0-7787-2564-0 (paperback).--ISBN 978-1-4271-8092-6 (html)

        1. Earhart, Amelia, 1897-1937--Juvenile literature.
2. Women air pilots--United States--Biography--Juvenile literature. I. Title. II. Series: Crabtree groundbreaker biographies

TL540.E3D35 2016   j629.13092   C2015-908716-3
                                                          C2015-908717-1

Library of Congress Cataloging-in-Publication Data

CIP available at Library of Congress

Crabtree Publishing Company

www.crabtreebooks.com   1-800-387-7650

Printed in Canada/022016/IH20151223

Published in Canada
Crabtree Publishing
616 Welland Ave.
St. Catharines, Ontario
L2M 5V6

Published in the United States
Crabtree Publishing
PMB16A
350 Fifth Ave., Suite 3308
New York, NY 10118

Published in the United Kingdom
Crabtree Publishing
Maritime House
Basin Road North, Hove
BN41 1WR

Published in Australia
Crabtree Publishing
386 Mt. Alexander Rd.
Ascot Vale (Melbourne)
VIC 3032

Contents

HAMMOND·Y

DEPARTMENT OF COMMERC
BUREAU OF AIR COMMERCE

Above: In this 1936 photo, famed aviator Amelia Earhart helps promote the newly formed Bureau of Air Commerce. The U.S. government created this agency to help improve aviation safety, as well as control air traffic, during a time when air travel was becoming increasingly popular.

Above right: Amelia drew crowds wherever she went. In this photo, taken around 1932, a group gathers around her as she strolls near the Lockheed Vega in which she became the first woman to fly solo across the Atlantic.

Chapter 1
Talking the Talk

On June 17, 1928, Amelia Earhart and two male aviators took off from Trepassey, Newfoundland, on the east coast of Canada. Twenty hours and 49 minutes later, they set their floatplane named *Friendship* down on the other side of the Atlantic Ocean. This was a big deal. With that flight, 30-year-old Amelia became the first woman to cross the Atlantic in an airplane. Strangely, not a soul was on hand to meet her and her fellow fliers when they landed. "Having crossed the Atlantic by air, we waited for the village to come out and greet us," said Amelia. It would be hours before anyone paid attention to the crew, or the floating aircraft.

Amelia Earhart in her headgear, a few days before her first transatlantic flight in June 1928.

Instant Fame

Even though Amelia's Atlantic crossing was a major milestone in international aviation, nobody took any notice of the airplane when it landed. None of the townsfolk seemed to recognize the historic importance of the occasion.

The problem was that Amelia's plane wasn't supposed to have landed in this particular area. "Probably our craft looked no more exciting than any other seaplane," said Amelia at the time.

Because of blinding fog, rain, and clouds, she and her companions had overshot their intended destination by about 350 miles (560 kilometers).

A Port in a Storm
(and Other Emergencies)

The coast of Newfoundland and Labrador, Canada, is the most easterly point in North America. Because of that, it has been a safe haven for transatlantic air travelers for more than a century. It has also been the launch point—or a port-of-call—on at least ten historic flights (and flight attempts) across the Atlantic, including both of Amelia's transatlantic flights.

From the 1940s until the early 1960s, Gander Airport in Newfoundland was a final refueling stop for commercial airlines heading overseas. After longer-range aircraft were developed, flights no longer needed to stop for a fill-up.

Newfoundland also has a long history of helping aircraft pilots and passengers in emergency situations. The best-known example happened following the terrorist attacks in the United States on September 11, 2001. On that day, following the hijackings and crashes of four passenger planes, including the ones that resulted in the collapse of New York's World Trade Center, aircraft were forbidden to enter U.S. airspace. More than 200 planes that were already in flight were diverted to airports in Canada. Of the 53 that were sent to Newfoundland, 38 landed in the small town of Gander. More than 6,000 passengers and almost 500 crewmembers were stranded there for a week. The people of Gander opened their homes and their hearts to the tired travelers.

They were supposed to be in Ireland. Instead, they had set down in the small town of Burry Port, Wales.

Eventually, a few curious local boaters approached the floating aircraft. When they discovered who was on board, news spread like wildfire! In no time, thousands of townspeople flocked to the seashore. They wanted to see Amelia Earhart, the first woman to cross the Atlantic by air.

"When ... Miss Earhart [came] ashore, she was the recipient of so enthusiastic a reception by the 2,000 inhabitants of this town that it seemed for a few minutes as if she would not outlive her triumph," stated a *New York Times* article.

Amelia and the two men spent a night in Burry Port before flying to Southampton, England, for an official welcome to Britain.

Amelia and a crewmate stand on one of the pontoons with which the Friendship *was outfitted for its transatlantic flight.*

Women Take Flight

By the time Amelia Earhart took to the skies, women had been flying for more than 100 years. Two different French women are credited with being the first female to pilot an aircraft. Was it Jeanne Garnerin or Sophie Blanchard? Both piloted hot air balloons in France in the early 1800s, and both have other claims to aviation fame. Jeanne was the first woman to make a parachute jump (1799), and Sophie was the first woman to earn her living as an aviator. She was also the first woman in history to be killed in an aviation accident. In 1819, her balloon caught fire and crashed, and Sophie fell to her death.

In this illustration from a Parisian fashion magazine published in the 1870s, French balloonist Jeanne Garnerin is shown rising above a crowd of spectators in a hot air balloon in March 1802. Several years earlier, Jeanne had become the first female to ascend in a balloon without a male pilot.

MORT DE Mᵐᵉ BLANCHARD (1819)

The death of French balloonist Sophie Blanchard is shown in one of a series of trading cards that depicted events in ballooning and parachuting in the 1800s.

A century later, another French woman, Thérèse Peltier, became the first woman to pilot an airplane. She only flew 650 feet (200 meters), and the plane was only eight feet (2.5 m) off the ground. But she did it! That was in 1908, just five years after the Wright Brothers had invented the airplane.

Thérèse Peltier

Two years later, yet another French woman, Raymonde de Laroche, became the first woman in the world to earn a flying license.

Over the next 50 years, the world witnessed women achieving many "firsts" in the air—the first female to use aerobatic, or stunt-flying, skills (1915), movie stunt pilot (1929), and glider pilot (1931); the first female commercial airline pilot (1934), military pilots (1942), and helicopter pilot (1947).

Raymonde de Laroche

In 1963, Valentina Tereshkova of the Soviet Union became the first female astronaut. American Sally Ride was the first woman to become a U.S. astronaut when the Space Shuttle *Challenger* launched in June 1983. In 1999, Lt. Col. Eileen Collins became the first woman to pilot a Space Shuttle.

Valentina Tereshkova

Sally Ride

Eileen Collins

In Southampton, reporters, photographers, officials, and thousands of fans greeted the trio. The only one of the fliers anyone cared about, though, was Amelia. She became an overnight, international celebrity because of the voyage.

"It was genuinely surprising what a disproportion of attention was given to the woman member of the crew at the expense of the men," Amelia wrote in her book, *The Fun of It*.

It particularly surprised her because she hadn't so much as touched the controls of the plane during the transatlantic flight.

Although Amelia was a licensed pilot, she had no experience with this particular type of aircraft. That meant she was unable to fly it. She had merely been invited along for the ride—and for the publicity a woman's presence on the voyage would generate.

All the attention embarrassed Amelia. She tried to set the record straight every chance she got. "I was just baggage, like a sack of potatoes," she told a reporter the day after the flight.

She quickly added: "Maybe someday I'll try it alone."

Four years later, Amelia did just that. In 1932, she became the first woman—and just the second person ever—to fly solo across the Atlantic Ocean.

> *"Ever since my first crossing in the* Friendship *in 1928, when I was merely a passenger, I have wanted to attempt a solo flight."*
>
> Amelia Earhart, in *The Fun of It*

Amelia Earhart poses in front of the propeller of the Lockheed Electra 10E aircraft that she used during her attempted round-the-world flight in 1937. As well as being an aviation pioneer, Amelia inspired women and girls to become independent and pursue goals that had once been unimaginable in their lives and work. She even influenced how they dressed!

Superstar in the Sky

By the time Amelia crossed the Atlantic the second time, she was already one of the world's best-known pilots. That's largely because her husband, George Putnam, was a world-class promoter. From the minute he met Amelia, George did everything he could do to keep her name in lights. He arranged for her to make lecture tours, promote products, write books, and have her photo taken with celebrities.

That's not to say Amelia didn't deserve fame. During the early 1930s, she took risks and set record after record in the air. She was awarded a Gold Medal from the National Geographic Society and the Distinguished Flying Cross from the United States Army Air Corps. The French government gave her the Cross of Knight of the Legion of Honor.

AMELIA'S ASSOCIATES

Amelia Earhart was neither the first nor the best female pilot in America. She was, however, the one with the best publicist—her husband George Putnam. In her day, she shared the skies with a number of other women who were flying as high, fast, and far as Amelia, including the following:

- The first American woman to become a licensed pilot was Harriet Quimby in 1911. Born in Michigan in 1875, Harriet was also the first woman to fly across the English Channel. Ten weeks later, on July 1, 1912, she died after being accidentally ejected from her plane during an air meet in Boston.

Harriet Quimby

- Ruth Nichols earned her pilot's license at age 23. In 1928, she was co-pilot on the first-ever non-stop flight from New York to Miami, Florida. Along with Amelia, she raced in the first air race for women in 1929. Ruth didn't cross the finish line because she crashed her plane during the race. During her flying career, she set seven records for speed, distance, and altitude. In 1932, wrote Amelia, "Ruth has been, to date, officially higher, faster and farther in a straight line than any other woman." Ruth died of a drug overdose in 1960, at age 59.

Ruth Nichols

- In 1928, 16-year-old Elinor Smith got her pilot's license, making her the youngest certified pilot in the world. By then, she had already been flying for eight years! She made her first solo flight at 15. When she was 17, "she attracted plenty of attention—and trouble for herself—by flying under all the East River bridges [in New York City] one Sunday afternoon," wrote Amelia of her friend. During her career, Elinor set many records for altitude and endurance. In 1934, she also became the first woman to appear on the Wheaties cereal box. Elinor died in 2010 at the age of 98.

Elinor Smith

- Twenty-three-year-old Louise Thaden won the first-ever Women's Air Derby in 1929. That same year, she also set a women's endurance record, by flying for 22 hours without stopping. Three years later, she broke that record, flying for 196 hours straight. That's eight days in the sky without stopping! In 1936, Louise (with Blanche Noyes as co-pilot) became the first woman to win an air race in which men and women competed together. She set a speed record during the race. Louise died in 1979, just before her 74th birthday.

Louise Thaden

- In 1929, Blanche Noyes gave up acting to become an aviator. That same year, during the Women's Air Derby race from Santa Monica, California, to Cleveland, her plane caught fire. She put out the fire in midair, crash landed, and resumed the race once repairs to her plane were made. Like Amelia, she joined the Bureau of Air Commerce in 1936, and for years after World War II was the only female pilot to fly U.S. government planes. Blanche died in 1981 at the age of 81.

Blanche Noyes (right)
and Amelia Earhart

- In 1930, Laura Ingalls, whom Amelia called an "aerial acrobat," performed 980 loops in a row! It took her three-and-a-quarter hours, and she earned one dollar for each loop she performed. Later that year, she set a world barrel roll record, performing 714 in a row. She later became the first American woman to fly over the Andes mountains, the first person to fly solo around South America, and the first woman to fly from North America to South America. Laura died in 1967 at age 73.

Laura Ingalls

FLIGHT LOG

In Amelia Earhart's day, female pilots were rare. They were the subject of much discussion and curiosity. Amelia was often asked: "What are women flyers like? What do they do when not flying? How do they look?"

Her answer? "They are simply thoroughly normal girls and women who happen to have taken up flying rather than golf, swimming or steeplechasing [a form of horse racing]."

Amelia was also the first president of the Ninety-Nines, a flying organization for female pilots. She was the first female officer elected to the National Aeronautic Association, and she promoted aviation for women whenever she could throughout her career.

Amelia Earhart was a feminist before "feminism" was even a commonly used word. She lived in a time when the only careers open to women were teaching, typing, and nursing. As a woman in a non-traditional occupation, she was idolized by many young women of the day.

Amelia encouraged women to wear pants (instead of skirts) if they felt like it, to study sciences and auto mechanics if that's where their interests lay, and to remain single and independent if that's what they chose to do. "When you graduate, be sure you go on and have a career," she told female university students. "Don't get married as soon as you get out of school."

This portrait photo of Amelia, taken in 1930, could as easily have appeared in a fashion magazine as in an aviation publication.

Throughout her life, Amelia's independence, courage, and determination were considered by some to be "unladylike" qualities. At the same time, she was charming, poised, and stylish—undeniably feminine. This combination of qualities gave her universal appeal.

As Amelia's aviation career took off, so did her international popularity. She became a superstar celebrity, as famous in her day as the rock stars and sports heroes of today.

At the peak of her fame, Amelia vanished over the Pacific Ocean while attempting to set another aviation record. The world that loved her went into shock. Her disappearance remains one of the greatest unsolved mysteries of the 20th century.

As a little girl growing up in a small town in Kansas, Amelia had a huge imagination—but even she could not have imagined the impact she would make on the world.

A U.S. air mail stamp honoring Amelia was issued in 1963.

FLYING INTO HISTORY

The first person to design a workable flying machine was Leonardo da Vinci in 1485. The concept for his *ornithopter*, which was never built, was similar to that of modern-day helicopters. While Leonardo's machine never got off the ground, the Montgolfier brothers' hot air balloon did. It took off for the first time in France in 1793.

In 1804, a British inventor flew a glider, an aircraft without an engine, for the first time. A German engineer improved on that design in 1891, creating a more practical glider. That same year, an American astronomer designed an airplane that used steam power, but it was too heavy to get off the ground.

After studying these previous designs, American brothers Orville and Wilbur Wright built the first gas-powered airplane. The *Flyer*, as they called it, took off on December 17, 1903. The craft was too heavy, though, so the brothers went back to the drawing board. In October 1905, *Flyer III* took to the air. Wilbur flew it for 39 minutes, until it ran out of gas. This was the first flight of what the Wrights called an aircraft of "practical utility."

It's hard to say who invented the helicopter. Many people designed many different versions of it in the late 19th and early 20th centuries. The one that most closely resembles helicopters of today was invented in the United States in 1939 by a Russian-born engineer named Igor Sikorsky.

Perhaps the most famous photograph of the flight by Wilbur and Orville Wright of their Flyer *craft, on December 17, 1903, at Kitty Hawk, North Carolina. Orville is lying on the plane while controlling it, and Wilbur is running alongside after steadying the craft.*

Chapter 2
Head in the Clouds

When Amelia Earhart was a child, girls were supposed to read, sew, and learn to cook. They were to be clean and quiet, and wear pretty dresses. They weren't supposed to engage in sports, catch bugs, or get their clothes dirty. "Unfortunately, I lived at a time when girls were still girls," wrote Amelia in *The Fun of It*. Fortunately for Amelia—and for the world—her parents tossed aside society's rules. They allowed their daughter the freedom to explore, experiment, and play "boys' games." They allowed her to fly free.

Early Independence

Amelia Mary Earhart was born in her grandparents' house in Atchison, Kansas, on July 24, 1897. It was the house where Amelia's mother, Amy, had been raised. Although Amy had moved out of Atchison by the time Amelia was born, Amy's parents wanted her to come home so they could care for her during the pregnancy. And so baby Amelia was born in her mother's childhood bedroom.

Amelia's birthplace: her grandparents' home in Atchison, Kansas.

Left: Amy Otis, shown here with daughter Amelia following Amelia's 1928 flight as the first woman to fly across the Atlantic, claimed to have been the first woman to climb Pikes Peak in Colorado (above), one of the highest summits in the Rocky Mountains, in 1890. This story may have served to inspire her daughter to reach for the skies. Amy's claim was not true, however. She did reach the top of the mountain in 1890, but Julie Archibald Holmes was the first woman to conquer Pikes Peak, in 1858.

Amy's parents had been among the early settlers of Atchison, located on the banks of the Missouri River. Amy's father was a lawyer and judge, her mother an upper-class woman with big-city roots, born in Philadelphia, Pennsylvania. They were wealthy, meaning that Amy—and her seven siblings—had a privileged youth and childhood. Amy attended private school, had servants, and owned her own horses. She was also an accomplished mountain climber!

When Amy was 21, her parents threw her a coming-out party, a grand soirée designed to formally introduce the young lady into high society. At the party, Amy Otis met law student Edwin Earhart. The two quickly fell in love and wanted to marry.

Amy's father disapproved of Edwin, who traveled in the wrong social circles and had no money. Amy's father wanted "better" for his daughter. He refused to consent to the couple marrying until Edwin had graduated law school and found a good job in a law firm. He hoped that, by then, Amy would give up on marrying the young man.

His plan didn't work, and five years later, Amy and Edwin were wed. They set up house in Kansas City, Kansas, about 50 miles (80 km) south of Atchison.

Two years later, little Amelia was born.

For the first three years of her life, Amelia lived happily with her parents in an ordinary home in Kansas City. When her sister Muriel was born, though, everything changed.

Her mother was unable to cope with the demands of two small children. At the same time, Amelia's grandmother, "Grandmother Otis," was grieving the loss of three close family members. To lessen Amy's workload and to cheer up the lonely senior, Amelia was sent to Atchison to live with Grandmother Otis. "I was lent to her for company during the winter months," Amelia wrote.

"Highly independent and precocious— that's our baby."

Amy Earhart, describing her daughter Amelia

A portrait of Amelia as a young girl.

For the next seven years, the little girl spent ten months a year in Atchison. There, she attended a small, private school, excelling in all her subjects. Only when school was out for summers did she go to Kansas City to be with her parents and her sister.

Grandmother Otis did not approve of Amelia's "unladylike" behavior and scolded her for doing such things as hopping fences. That didn't stop the child from exploring caves, sledding, hunting snakes, riding horses, and participating in "mud ball fights." It just meant Amelia worked hard to hide her more adventurous activities from her grandmother.

Amelia's parents, on the other hand, encouraged both of their daughters to be athletic, carefree, and active, regardless of whether what they did was considered "ladylike." The girls spent their summers exploring and playing together. Edwin went fishing with them and let them stay up late to watch an eclipse of the Moon. Amelia particularly loved basketball, bicycling, and tennis.

Edwin also bought Amelia and Muriel toys that were more typically intended for boys. One Christmas, the girls asked for footballs because "we have plenty of baseballs, bats, etc." The girls got their footballs. They also got a small rifle that they used to shoot rats in a barn.

One summer, mother Amy sewed bloomers for her daughters to play in. Bloomers are poufy shorts gathered at the knee. At the time, it was scandalous for girls to wear anything but skirts or dresses. "We wore [the bloomers] Saturdays to play in," wrote Amelia. "And though we felt

terribly free and athletic, we also felt somewhat as outcasts among the little girls who fluttered about us in their skirts."

As active as the girls were, they also loved to read. Amelia devoured the works of the great 19th-century novelists, such as Charles Dickens, Sir Walter Scott, and George Eliot (who was really a British woman named Mary Ann Evans). She read magazines, "western thrillers," and "medieval romances."

> "Books have meant much to me. Not only did I myself read considerably, but Mother read aloud to my sister and me, early and late. So fundamental became the habit that on occasions when we girls had to do housework, instead of both pitching in and doing it together, one was selected to read aloud and the other to work."
>
> Amelia Earhart, *The Fun of It*

Changes in the Air

By the time Amelia was six years old, her father's law practice was failing. Edwin may have been charming and intelligent enough to be a successful lawyer, but he didn't apply himself to his trade. In 1903, the family ran out of money.

Edwin decided to change careers and become an inventor. Having been a lawyer for a railroad company for many years, he knew all about trains—and he saw an opportunity in that industry. He put all his energy into designing a flag holder for the signal flags that flew on a train's caboose, or last car.

Edwin believed this invention would make him rich. Instead, when he was ready to sell it to the railroad companies, he discovered that someone else had invented the same thing two years earlier. It was "a terrible blow" to him when he heard the news. He was forced to return to the law, the only thing he was trained to do.

For the next five years, Edwin managed to earn small amounts of money doing legal work here and there. But the family barely got by.

Finally, when Amelia was 11 years old, in the summer of 1908, her father got a job with the Chicago, Rock Island and Pacific Railroad. It was a low-level job, but it was a job Edwin desperately needed. It was also a job that required the family to move to Des Moines, Iowa, about 200 miles (320 km) north of Atchison.

The move was hard on Amelia. She left behind everything, and everyone, she had ever known. She went from living a privileged life with Grandmother Otis—in a small town where she knew everyone—to living an unsettled existence in a larger, unknown city.

During the Earharts' four years in Des Moines, they lived in four different homes. Every time Edwin's salary increased, he moved his family into a bigger and fancier house. Finally, the family settled in an upscale part of town, where the best-known members of Des Moines society lived.

Amy and Edwin hired servants. They bought lovely clothes for their daughters. They attended concerts and visited art galleries. They socialized with upper-class society.

All the while, Edwin continued to rise

FLIGHT LOG

In the summer of 1908, when the Earhart family first moved to Des Moines, Edwin took Amelia to the Iowa State Fair. There, she saw an airplane for the first time. It was just four and a half years after the Wright Brothers first flew an airplane, so this one wasn't fancy. And it didn't interest Amelia in the least. "It was a thing of rusty wire and wood and not at all interesting," she said later.

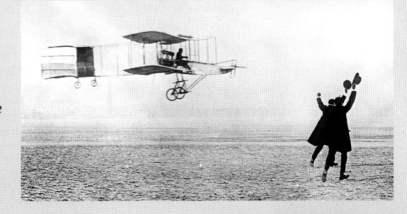

This biplane, photographed in France in 1908, was similar to the kind of plane that Amelia first saw at the Iowa State Fair.

through the railroad company ranks. Eventually, he earned the privilege of traveling in the company's private rail car when he took business trips. The luxurious carriage had a kitchen, dining room, and sleeping berths, or beds. It even came with its own chef!

Whenever he took long trips, Edwin took Amy, Amelia, Muriel, and their maid along for the ride. It was an exciting, extravagant time in Amelia's life. Little did she know, though, that it would mark the end of her childhood happiness.

Spiraling Downward

When Amelia was 14 years old, her world fell apart. Her father, who had always enjoyed an occasional glass of whisky, began drinking heavily. He often arrived home drunk. He stopped playing with his daughters, who began to fear him. He flew into rages, once raising his hand to hit Amelia. Thankfully, her mother stepped in to stop him from hurting the child. In 1911, Edwin packed up and left his family, only to return a few months later—for the sake of the girls.

In early 1912, Amelia's world further crumbled when her beloved Grandmother Otis died. Shortly after that, her home life took another downward turn when her father lost his job because of his alcoholism.

It would be a year before Edwin found another position—and when he did, it meant another move for the family. This time, the Earharts moved north to St. Paul, Minnesota, where Edwin worked as a lowly railroad clerk. There, his drinking worsened. He broke promises to his daughters, regularly came home drunk, and did not earn enough money to support his family. Amelia's grades at school dropped dramatically because of the stress in her home life.

After a year in St. Paul, Edwin was fired again, meaning the family was to be uprooted once more.

In the spring of 2014, the Earharts moved to Springfield, Missouri, where Edwin believed there was a job waiting for him. When they arrived at the Springfield train station, they discovered there was no job. The family had nothing left, and nowhere to go.

For Amy Earhart, it was the last straw. The next day, she packed up her daughters and took them to Chicago to live with friends. Edwin returned to St. Paul alone. Later, he would move back to Kansas City to restart his law career.

> "I went to at least six high schools but managed to graduate in the usual four years' time. The last one was Hyde Park in Chicago, and it furnished a diploma."
>
> Amelia Earhart,
> *The Fun of It*

Amelia Takes Flight

In Chicago, Amelia attended the best public high school in the city. Hyde Park High School was known for its wide variety of extracurricular activities, excellent sports facilities (for girls and boys), and top-notch academics. It was the perfect place for a bright, active, and adventurous student like Amelia. Despite everything available to her, though, Amelia did not join in. She made no friends and did not participate in clubs or sports. She spent her spare time in the library by herself. She was lonely, unhappy, and worried about her family.

Still, Amelia managed to pass all her courses and graduate from high school in June 1915.

That fall, Amelia's parents reunited, and the whole family moved back to Kansas City. For a year after that, "I waited around," wrote Amelia. She didn't work or attend classes during that time. Finally, her mother convinced her to go to the Ogontz School near Philadelphia, where she had relatives.

Ogontz was a "finishing school" where young women were prepared to enter society. Academic courses were offered, but the school had a strong focus on such things as social graces and etiquette. Students were schooled in culture and the fine arts, and were required to participate in exercise programs, but marriage was still seen as a primary goal for the young women.

Ogontz was a place of discipline, schedules, and high expectations—and it was a good choice for Amelia. She excelled there. At the beginning of her second year, she was voted class vice president. She also took leadership roles in a number of clubs.

During her Christmas vacation in 1917, 20-year-old Amelia visited Toronto, where her sister Muriel was studying to become a teacher.

By this time, Canada had been actively involved in World War I for three years. The United States, on the other hand, had joined the fighting only a few months earlier. In Toronto, Amelia saw many wounded men who had returned from the war—the sorts of casualties that hadn't yet been seen in the United States. Said Amelia:

"Honor is the foundation of courage."

The motto Amelia chose for her class at Ogontz

"There for the first time, I realized what the World War meant. Instead of new uniforms and brass bands, I saw only the results of a [three] years' desperate struggle; men without arms and legs, men who were paralyzed and men who were blind."

Flight Log

While Amelia was a student at Ogontz School in Philadelphia, sh started a scrapbook. She called it "Activities of Women" and fille newspapers clippings about remarkable women doing unconve things. The book included articles about such high-achieving wo a film producer, a bank president, an engineer, a fire lookout, pc and a police commissioner. Amelia appreciated them for their " fascinating lives."

Amelia was shocked by what she saw. She knew she had to stay in Toronto to help. "I can't bear the thought of going back to school and being so useless," she wrote to her mother.

Amelia quit her studies at Ogontz, moved to Toronto, and became a volunteer assistant nurse. Her duties included everything from making beds and scrubbing floors to serving meals, dispensing medication, and playing tennis with recovering soldiers.

A nurse with a group of wounded World War I surgical patients in 1918. Scenes such as this moved 20-year-old Amelia to leave her studies and move to Toronto, where she helped veterans like these as a nurse's aide.

In her spare time, Amelia rode horses near the city's airfields, which were abuzz with military aviation activity. This is where her fascination for flying took off:

"Though I had seen one or two [airplanes] at county fairs before, I now saw many of them as the officers were trained at the various fields around the city. Of course no civilian had [the] opportunity of going up. But I hung around in [my] spare time and absorbed all I could."

Amelia stayed in Toronto until the war ended in November 1918. By then, the 21-year-old nurse's aide was so run down and overworked that she became seriously ill with flu and pneumonia. She spent two months in the hospital, and it would be a year before she recovered enough to go back to school. She passed the time during her recuperation reading, learning to play the banjo, and taking an auto mechanics course.

IA'S LIFELONG ILLNESS

ut with flu and pneumonia in 1918 left her with a severe
her sinuses. The infection resulted in searing pain in the cavities
cheekbones. Antibiotics had not yet been discovered, meaning
re" for Amelia at the time was surgery to open up and clean
ses. The treatments, which were repeated several times over a
onths, left her so weak, it took her a year to recover. Even after
uses were never fully clear. Amelia suffered agonizing sinus
or the rest of her life.

Nursing wounded soldiers in Toronto had sparked "a yen for medicine" in Amelia. So, after recovering from her own illness, she enrolled in pre-med courses at Columbia University in New York City. Her goal was to become a physician.

Amelia started school in the fall of 1919. By then, her father Edwin had, once again, quit drinking. He was planning a move from Kansas City to Los Angeles, California, to start a new law practice. He wanted his whole family to come with him.

Amelia didn't join the family right away, insisting on continuing her education at Columbia. At this point in history, though, young, unmarried women still did what their parents told them to do—and Amelia's parents told her they wanted her in California. At the end of her first year at Columbia, "I yielded to their demands and headed to California," she said, adding that she had "the full intention of returning to Columbia in the fall."

Bitten by the Flying Bug

In the end, Amelia did not return to Columbia University. Instead, "aviation caught me," she wrote. During the summer and fall of 1920, she attended every "air circus," or flying exhibition, she could find. She dragged her father Edwin along with her every time.

Because flying had become the latest rage, and the California weather was usually clear and sunny, there were flying meets every

RULES OF CONDUCT

In the early 20th century, women like Amelia Earhart were rare. Playing sports was considered unladylike, and an interest in aviation was unheard of. The only jobs deemed appropriate for women were teaching, secretarial work, and nursing. Women were supposed to get married, raise children, and appear quietly by their husbands' sides. They were also restricted in their choices of clothing and activities.

Fortunately, there were some women like Amelia who believed women should have the same rights as men. Unfortunately, it took a world war to start them on the path.

From 1914–1918 (1917–1918 in the United States), most men were away from home, fighting in the war. That meant women took jobs that were previously unavailable to them. When the war ended, there was no turning back. While many women returned to their traditional roles, others fought to keep their new jobs and newfound freedom to choose their own paths in life.

Around the same time, after years of struggle, women around the world were finally starting to get the right to vote. In Canada, most women got the vote for federal, or national, elections in 1918. In the United States, the right of women to vote nationally was approved in 1920. Women in the United Kingdom were granted the vote in 1928.

During World War I, American women replaced male workers who were at war, performing jobs that had previously been done only by men. Top: Members of a Pennsylvania unit of the Women's Land Army take a break from working on a farm. Bottom: A female worker welds a "water jacket," designed to keep machine guns from overheating.

weekend in Los Angeles. By December, Amelia had put aside her dreams of becoming a doctor.

On December 28, 1920, she and her father attended yet another air show—this time at Long Beach. They returned to the airfield the next day, after Amelia convinced Edwin to pay for her to take a short flight. He wasn't keen on the idea, but he agreed. He paid pilot Frank Hawks $10 to take Amelia for a 10-minute flight over Los Angeles. "I am sure he thought one ride would be enough for me," Amelia said later, "and he might as well act to cure me promptly."

Of course, the flight had the opposite effect on the young woman. "As soon as we left the ground, I knew I myself had to fly."

INTRODUCING AMELIA TO THE AIR

The pilot who took Amelia Earhart up in a plane for the first time was Frank Hawks (shown here with the Texaco-sponsored "Sky-Chief" craft in which he set many flying records). He was the same age as Amelia, but he had learned to fly as a teenager. He had also served as a pilot during World War I. After the war, Frank made his living by taking customers for short plane rides, teaching flying, and flying daredevil "wing-walkers," people who, literally, walked on the wings of airplanes in flight.

After he introduced Amelia to the skies, he went on to set many speed and distance records in the air. He was once called "the fastest airman in the world." He died in a plane crash in 1938.

Chapter 3
Eye on the Sky

Amelia Earhart's parents did not approve of their daughter's wish to fly. They thought piloting an airplane was dangerous, and an unsuitable hobby for a young lady. They refused to give her money for her lessons—but that didn't stop the 23-year-old future flier. "My father thought if he did not pay, I would not fly," said Amelia. "But I was determined, and got my first job … to pay for the lessons I dearly wanted."

Into the Wild Blue Yonder

Amelia couldn't wait to start her flight training, and she knew she would be more comfortable with a female instructor. However, there was only one female flying instructor in all of Southern California at the time—a young woman named Anita Snook. Amelia decided that this pilot, known as "Neta," would be her teacher.

This photo shows Anita "Neta" Snook, Amelia's first flight instructor, as a student at the Davenport (Iowa) Aviation School in 1917. Seated sixth from the left in the front row, Neta was the only female student at the school.

Luckily for Amelia, Neta was based at Kinner Field, on the east side of Los Angeles. It would mean a long bus ride and a long walk to get to the airfield for lessons, but it was possible—and Amelia was determined.

Within days of her first flight with Frank Hawks, she ventured out to Kinner Field. Amelia marched up to Neta and got right to the point. "I want to learn to fly, and I understand you teach students," she said. "Will you teach me?"

Neta was impressed with Amelia's confidence and agreed to give her flying lessons. She also helped Amelia convince her parents that flying was safe and not unladylike. Neta even agreed to a monthly payment plan—rather than being paid up front—because Amelia had no money.

On January 3, 1921, Amelia showed up for her first lesson wearing her horse-riding clothes, the closest thing she had to flying gear. "From then on, my family scarcely saw me," she wrote. "I worked all the week and spent what I had of Saturday and Sunday at the airport."

At first, Amelia took her lessons in Neta's plane, a Canadian aircraft called a Canuck. The airplane had been used to train pilots during World War I. After the war ended, Neta purchased the plane and rebuilt it herself.

The Canuck was a biplane, with double wings and two cockpits, one behind the other. During flying lessons, the student would sit in the front cockpit, with Neta behind. Each cockpit had its own set of controls, so if need be, Neta could take charge of the plane and override student errors.

Amelia didn't like the Canuck. She thought it was clunky, slow, and underpowered. Within six months—against Neta's advice—she bought

AMELIA'S FIRST TEACHER

Anita "Neta" Snook's fascination with all things mechanical started when she was a child. She loved boats, cars, and airplanes. In college, she took courses in mechanics, machinery repair, and auto maintenance. In 1917, she became the first female student to attend the famous Curtiss School of Aviation in Virginia. However, early in 1918, the United States government banned all non-military flying until World War I ended. Neta's flight school days were over before she'd even soloed, or flown alone.

After the war, Neta bought a damaged warplane called a Canuck. Using the mechanical skills she had gained over the years, she rebuilt it. Then she taught herself to fly. From then on, she made her living in the air—giving lessons, taking passengers for rides, and testing new aircraft.

Neta became Amelia Earhart's first flying teacher in January 1921. A month later, Neta became the first woman to enter a "men's" flying race in Los Angeles. She came in fifth.

In 1922, Neta got married, had a baby, and gave up flying. She remained out of the public eye until 1974, when she wrote her autobiography, called *I Taught Amelia to Fly*. Neta died in 1991 at the age of 95.

Neta Snook at Kinner Field, Los Angeles, in 1921.

herself a smaller, lighter, peppier aircraft called a Kinner Airster. Its smaller size meant it was more maneuverable, but it also meant it was unstable. It was not an aircraft designed for beginners. Neta didn't trust the plane, and she didn't trust Amelia's abilities to fly it.

A Kinner Airster, similar to the one Amelia bought in 1921.

In general, Amelia's flying skills made Neta nervous. She felt Amelia was overly confident, a trait that could lead to potentially dangerous mistakes.

By this time, Amelia's mother and sister had come to support Amelia's love of flying. They pooled their savings to help Amelia come up with the $2,000 she needed to purchase the Airster. Amelia bought the little plane in July 1921 and named it the *Canary* because of its bright yellow paint job.

Despite her concerns about plane and pilot, Neta agreed to continue Amelia's lessons, now using the *Canary* as the training vehicle. Before long, Neta's fears about the plane and Amelia's abilities were confirmed. During one of Amelia's first flights in the *Canary*, with Neta aboard as usual, she taxied the little plane

Amelia (right) and her flight instructor, Neta Snook, pose in front of the Canary, *the plane Amelia purchased secondhand in 1921.*

down the airstrip—and crashed it into the trees at the end of the runway.

The accident was thought to have been caused by a combination of mechanical malfunction and pilot inexperience. Fortunately, nobody was hurt, but the *Canary* needed some repair.

At this point, Amelia realized she needed training in how to *purposely* get into trouble in the air, so she could learn how to get out of trouble, before anything more serious happened. She knew Neta wasn't the person to teach her these skills.

She recruited former army pilot John Montijo for the job. John was also a stunt flier in the movies at the time, so Amelia knew he had the skills she needed. He taught her aerobatics, or "stunting" skills. Stunt flying training included what Amelia called the "three S's"—slips, stalls, and spins. Sometimes, it also included loops and barrel rolls.

Stunt flying is fun for pilots—but that's not the main goal of the training.

"A knowledge of some stunts is judged necessary to good flying," Amelia wrote in *The Fun of It.* "Unless a pilot has actually recovered from a stall, has actually put his plane into a spin and brought it out, he cannot know accurately what those acts entail."

John Montijo became a civilian instructor and stunt pilot after serving with the U.S. Army Air Corps in World War I. One condition of his taking Amelia Earhart as a student was that she become experienced in aerobatics as a way of preparing for emergency situations.

Fun with Purpose

Many flight schools teach aerobatics, or stunt flying, as part of their regular training programs. These are the sorts of tricks you see at air shows—planes performing loops, flying upside down, or zooming straight up in the air until they stall and plummet nose-first toward the ground. For daring and skilled pilots, these stunts may be fun, but they also have a purpose.

Many stunts started as military maneuvers that allowed pilots to dodge enemy planes in wartime. Others recreate emergencies that might happen in the air. It's important that pilots learn how to get in and out of these situations on purpose, so if something happens in the air, they know what to do.

All require strong stomachs and nerves of steel!

Shown here are diagrams of maneuvers that Amelia called the "three S's"—slips, stalls, and spins.

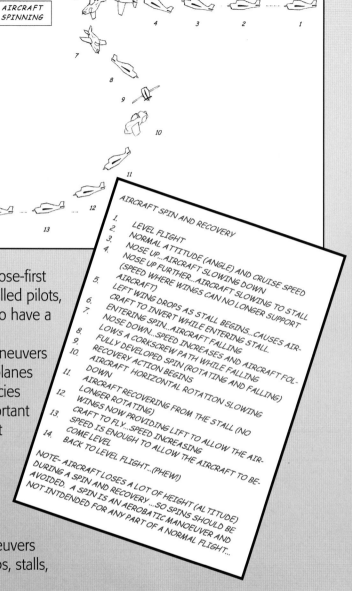

AIRCRAFT SPINNING

AIRCRAFT SPIN AND RECOVERY

1. LEVEL FLIGHT
2. NORMAL ATTITUDE (ANGLE) AND CRUISE SPEED
3. NOSE UP...AIRCRAFT SLOWING DOWN
4. NOSE UP FURTHER...AIRCRAFT SLOWING TO STALL (SPEED WHERE WINGS CAN NO LONGER SUPPORT AIRCRAFT)
5. LEFT WING DROPS AS STALL BEGINS...CAUSES AIRCRAFT TO INVERT WHILE ENTERING STALL.
6. ENTERING SPIN...AIRCRAFT ENTERING STALL.
7. NOSE DOWN...SPEED INCREASES AND AIRCRAFT FOLLOWS A CORKSCREW PATH WHILE FALLING
8. FULLY DEVELOPED SPIN (ROTATING AND FALLING)
9. RECOVERY ACTION BEGINS
10. AIRCRAFT HORIZONTAL ROTATION SLOWING DOWN
11. AIRCRAFT RECOVERING FROM THE STALL (NO LONGER ROTATING)
12. WINGS NOW PROVIDING LIFT TO ALLOW THE AIRCRAFT TO FLY...SPEED INCREASING
13. SPEED IS ENOUGH TO ALLOW THE AIRCRAFT TO BECOME LEVEL
14. BACK TO LEVEL FLIGHT...(PHEW!)

NOTE- AIRCRAFT LOSES A LOT OF HEIGHT (ALTITUDE) DURING A SPIN AND RECOVERY...SO SPINS SHOULD BE AVOIDED. A SPIN IS AN AEROBATIC MANOEUVER AND NOT INTDENDED FOR ANY PART OF A NORMAL FLIGHT...

Fame but No Fortune

The training Amelia did with John, plus the training she did with Neta, added up to enough experience to take an official flight test. On December 15, 1921, the Aero Club of America (ACA) evaluated Amelia's flying ability. It wasn't her best flight ever, but her performance was

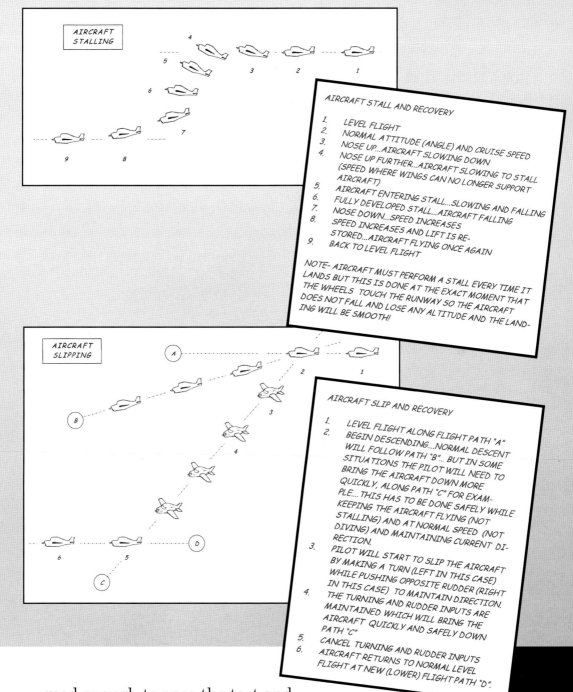

good enough to pass the test and
allow her to become a certified flier.

A year and a half later, Amelia became
the 16th woman in the world to earn an
international flying license from the Féderation
Aéronautique Internationale (FAI). She needed

License to Fly

In the early 20th century, American pilots did not need a license to fly, but if they chose to become licensed, the Aero Club of America (ACA) was the organization that would provide the certification. The ACA flight test consisted of flying a series of figure eights in the sky and performing two landings—one under power, the other a glide to earth with the engine shut off.

In 1922, the Aero Club, which had been founded in 1905, became the National Aeronautic Association (NAA). It continued to issue pilots' licenses until 1926, when the U.S. government took over certification of fliers.

The Féderation Aéronautique Internationale was a worldwide organization founded in 1905 by flight associations from eight nations, including the United States and Britain. Its goal was "to regulate the various aviation meetings [or exhibitions] and advance the science and sport of Aeronautics." If a pilot wanted to attempt an official record—for altitude, speed or distance—anywhere in the world, he or she needed an FAI license for the record to be recognized.

Flight Log

Before she'd earned her FAI license, Amelia had set an *unofficial* altitude record for female pilots, a record that was broken by a different pilot a month later. Amelia tried, but failed, to top the record again a few weeks later.

this license so she could officially attempt altitude, distance, and speed records in the air.

After she earned her ACA certification, Amelia began flying in exhibitions, so-called "air rodeos," or "air derbies." At these events, she did fly-pasts, raced with other female pilots, and performed aerobatic displays. As a rare female pilot, her presence always drew a crowd—and media attention.

Newspaper reporters began to interview Amelia about her adventures in the air. She was also featured in full-page advertisements for the

Kinner Airster. The plane's builder promoted the aircraft with a photo of Amelia, calling it "a lady's plane as well as a man's."

In August 1922, the *Los Angeles Examiner* published an article about Amelia, quoting her as saying she planned to fly across North America one day soon. Accompanying the article was a half-page photograph of Amelia in her leather flying jacket and goggles. The following

THE BEAUTY OF THE SKY

When Amelia began flying, few people had ever had the experience of soaring through the sky. In her book *The Fun of It*, she describes it for her readers.

She tells them "the sensation that accompanies [fear of] heights is seldom present." She assures them they won't die of a heart attack, and that landings are generally smooth. "The descent of the plane is much less noticeable than the dropping of a modern elevator." She warns that there may be "bumps" in the air because of high and low pressure areas, but few people get air sick. "Nervousness over the first ride is probably the greatest cause of air sickness," she wrote.

Then she tells her readers what she loves most about flying:

"If the visibility is good, the passenger seems to see the whole world. Colors stand out and the shades of the earth … form an endless magic carpet."

This view of Earth from above offers a dramatic illustration of Amelia's feeling that the colors, shades, and patterns of our planet "form an endless magic carpet" when seen from the air.

A contented-looking Amelia Earhart sitting in the cockpit of her Lockheed Electra 10E, sometime around 1936.

spring, Amelia made news again as one of two female pilots headlining an air exhibition that celebrated the opening of a new airport.

Despite all the attention paid to her, Amelia earned little money from her air shows. To support her flying habit, she worked a variety of jobs. She was a photographer, a mailroom clerk in a telephone company, and a stenographer, a type of secretary who takes notes using a system called shorthand. She even drove a gravel truck at one point, a most unusual job for a young woman in the 1920s.

Still, Amelia and her family barely made ends meet. After one particularly disastrous investment, the Earharts lost all their savings. They began taking in boarders to help pay the bills. Eventually, Amelia had no choice but to sell the *Canary* to raise money to help her struggling family.

FLIGHT LOG

The man who bought Amelia's *Canary* in June 1923 crashed the plane the first time he took it up. The pilot and his passenger died. The aircraft was destroyed.

Grounded

Amelia's life took yet another dramatic turn in the spring of 1924, when her father Edwin filed for divorce from her mother Amy. After moving to Los Angeles, Edwin had quit drinking and joined a religious organization that helped him straighten out his life once and for all. In doing so, he realized his marriage wasn't working.

ROMANCING AMELIA

In 1922, Amelia's family took in boarders to help earn money. One of those boarders was an engineering student named Sam Chapman. He was five years older than Amelia, and the two hit it off instantly. They played tennis together, discussed literature and philosophy, and shared progressive ideas about men's and women's roles in the world.

In 1924, Sam asked Amelia to marry him. She said yes, but no matter how he tried, she would not commit to a wedding date. Four years later, after she had become an international celebrity, Amelia suddenly broke up with Sam. The two remained friends for the rest of Amelia's life. Sam never married.

After the divorce, he stayed in California, but Amy, Muriel, and Amelia headed "home" to the East Coast. Muriel left first, taking a train to Boston, where she enrolled in summer school at Harvard University. Amelia decided she would return to Columbia University in the fall—but she wanted to take a little adventure first!

That summer, Amelia used some of the money she'd saved from selling the *Canary* to buy a bright yellow sports car. It was a 1923 Kissel Speedster "Goldbug" model.

This photo from an exhibit at an automotive museum shows a mannequin made up to look like Amelia sitting in the driver's seat of the yellow 1923 Kissel Speedster in which Amelia and her mom drove cross-country in 1924.

She and Amy packed up the colorful automobile and set out on a cross-country journey to Boston. Amy planned to stay there with Muriel, and Amelia would continue to New York City and Columbia University.

The 7,000-mile (11,000-km) trip took mother and daughter as far north as the Canadian Rockies, before they turned back south and east. They drove wherever their whims took them, exploring all the Canadian and American national parks they'd heard about but never visited. The journey took six weeks and was far more challenging than it would be today. At the time, most roads were unmarked and unpaved. Maps were inaccurate, and service stations offering gasoline and mechanical help were few and far between.

When they finally reached the East Coast, Amelia underwent emergency surgery. Her lifelong sinus problems had flared up again during the coast-to-coast drive.

After a few months' recovery, Amelia enrolled at Columbia as planned, but quit after just a few months because of the high cost. The only thing she could afford to do at this point in her life was move to Boston and stay with her mother and sister.

There, she tried a few part-time jobs and took the occasional academic course, but nothing Amelia did grabbed her interest.

"I finally reached Boston and had so many tourist stickers on the windshield there was little space left to see through it. When I parked the car, groups gathered to ask me questions about conditions of roads, how I'd come, why I'd come, and any number of other questions. The fact that my roadster was a cheerful canary color may have caused some of the excitement. It had been modest enough in California, but was a little outspoken for Boston."

Amelia Earhart,
The Fun of It

In the fall of 1926, when Amelia was 29 years old, she tried yet another part-time job, this time as a social worker at a place called Denison House. It was an institution that helped immigrants settle into their new lives in America. It provided English lessons, food and medical care, and activities for children and youths.

Amelia's first job at Denison House was teaching English to adults. She loved it—and the Denison House managers loved her. Within a year, Amelia was hired full time and put in charge of programs for pre-school children and school-aged girls.

Working full-time meant Amelia could afford to fly again. She joined the Boston branch of the National Aeronautic Association, eventually becoming its first-ever female officer. She served as a local sales rep for Kinner Airster planes and promoted aviation for women every chance she got.

Even though she no longer owned an aircraft, Amelia's connections with local pilots gave her opportunities to fly on occasion—and once again, as a rare female pilot, the local media paid attention. One newspaper called her "one of the best women pilots in the United States." Before long, Amelia was as famous in Boston as she had been in Los Angeles.

Little did she know that her local fame was about to explode into global stardom.

SIGNATURE HAIRDO

When Amelia began her flying lessons, she had waist-length hair. One day, a little girl told Amelia, "You don't look like an aviatrix [an outdated term for a female pilot]. You have long hair." It was true that most female fliers of the day had modern, short, easy-care hair. After that, Amelia began cutting her hair—just a little bit each night, so her mother wouldn't be shocked by the change. Once her blond hair had become a fashionably short bob, Amelia curled it every day. It appeared so naturally tousled and wind-blown that everyone thought it just grew that way! The haircut became part of Amelia's lifelong signature look.

Chapter 4
Flying to Fame

In May 1927, American pilot Charles Lindbergh made history when he became the first person to fly solo across the Atlantic Ocean. His flight from New York City to Paris took 33 hours, 30 minutes, making him an instant, international hero. Immediately, other fliers began planning to make the same trip—only they would do it faster, or they would fly in the opposite direction, or they would fly higher. The biggest "first" up for grabs at this point in aviation history, though, was to become the first woman to make the transatlantic flight.

Up, Up, and Away

One day in April 1928, Amelia Earhart received an out-of-the-blue telephone call while she was busy working at Denison House. On the other end of the line was former U.S. Navy officer and aviation adviser Captain Hinton H. Railey. He told Amelia he needed a female flier for a secret project. He had heard about Amelia through his connections in the piloting world.

Captain Railey asked Amelia a question that would change her life. "I inquired whether she'd like to participate in an important but hazardous flight," he said.

Amelia was curious to find out more, so she agreed to meet Captain Railey at his office that afternoon.

"Lucky Lindy"

Charles Lindbergh was born in Detroit, Michigan, in 1902. When he was 22 years old, he joined the U.S. Army, so he could become a pilot. He graduated from flight school a year later at the top of his class.

In May 1927, in a plane called *Spirit of St. Louis*, Charles became the first person to cross the Atlantic by air. He was showered with medals, awards, and honors for this feat of flight. He was also nicknamed "Lucky Lindy" at this time.

After his transatlantic flight, Charles focused his energy on promoting and developing aviation. In 1929, he married Anne Morrow and taught her to fly. The Lindberghs became well known for their globetrotting. Sadly, in 1932, they earned a different kind of fame, when their baby was kidnapped and killed.

Before and during World War II, Charles argued that the United States should stay out of the conflict with Nazi Germany. He even expressed admiration for certain elements of German culture. For these reasons, some people accused him of being a Nazi sympathizer.

Despite this controversy, Charles threw his support behind the U.S. war effort after Japan (an ally of Germany) attacked Pearl Harbor, Hawaii, on December 7, 1941.

During World War II, Charles flew 50 combat missions as a civilian flier, all of them in the Pacific, where the war effort was primarily directed against Japan. After the war, and for the rest of his life, he remained involved in aviation as a consultant. He also promoted environmental causes.

Charles Lindbergh died of cancer in 1974, at the age of 72.

Second Choice

Originally, another woman—a wealthy woman with zero flying experience—had decided that she would be the first woman to fly across the Atlantic. She would be a passenger, not a pilot. She would also fund the entire expedition.

In the end, her family begged her not to take the flight. Because this woman still wanted an American to be the first to woman to cross the Atlantic by air, she instructed her lawyer to find someone, "a lady, college-educated, attractive and, if possible, a flier."

Through a series of coincidences, Captain H. H. Railey heard about the lawyer's quest. He wanted to be part of the Atlantic expedition. Captain Railey tracked down the lawyer, then tracked down Amelia—and the flight was on!

As soon as he saw Amelia, the captain knew she was the right person for the mission he had in mind. "At sight, I was convinced that she was qualified," he said later. "I asked forthwith, 'How would you like to be the first woman to fly the Atlantic?'"

Amelia thought it over, "for one minute." Of course, her answer was yes!

Amelia was not trained in instrument flying, so she would not pilot the plane on the Atlantic crossing. Instead, she was to be "commander" of the flight, meaning she would

Flight Log

Other female pilots besides Amelia attempted to fly solo across the Atlantic following Charles Lindbergh's historic flight in 1927. Several died in the attempt. One pilot, Ruth Nichols, crashed her plane in Canada in 1931. She was planning another try when Amelia made her own historic flight.

make decisions about the voyage and maintain a log of the journey. Wilmer "Bill" Stultz would be the pilot, with mechanic Lou "Slim" Gordon on board as co-pilot.

The aircraft the team chose for the Atlantic crossing was a gold-and-orange Fokker F7 named the *Friendship*. It was equipped with the latest instruments, communication devices, and safety features. Its wheels were removed and replaced with pontoons, so it could land on water. The *Friendship* also carried extra gas tanks to fuel the long journey.

While the crewmembers prepared the *Friendship* in Boston, they kept their plans top-secret. They didn't want to be embarrassed if the flight failed to happen, and they didn't want to draw crowds that would interfere with

their work at the airfield. "And we didn't want to instigate a race," said Amelia, who stayed away from the airfield during preparations, to avoid gossip. She continued to work at Denison House, as if nothing unusual was going on in her life, although she did write farewell notes to her parents and her sister. These were to be delivered if she didn't survive the flight.

When the *Friendship* was ready to go, Amelia, Bill, and Slim flew the plane to Trepassey, Newfoundland, on the east coast of Canada. This was to be the starting point for their Atlantic crossing. The weather was against them, though, and the trio spent almost two weeks stranded in Trepassey, waiting for the fog, rain, and wind to clear.

Every time the weather looked promising, the crew hopped into the plane and attempted to take off. One day, they tried for four hours to lift the aircraft off the water, but the wind, tide, and waves kept them grounded.

On June 17, 1928, the weather cleared enough for another try. Again, the crew couldn't get the *Friendship* to lift off. In frustration, Amelia, Bill, and Slim decided they would have to lighten the plane's load if it was ever to become airborne. They dumped 200 gallons (760 liters) of gasoline—and tried again.

This time, the plane "rocked and staggered" as it plowed through the waves, but slowly, it managed to lift off. The plane circled the harbor once, and Amelia clicked the stopwatch to mark the start of their transatlantic flight!

The good news was that they were on their way—the bad news was they'd dumped so much fuel that now they barely had enough to cross the ocean. There was no room for error.

> *"We had made so many false starts, practically no one was on hand to see our real departure."*
>
> Amelia Earhart, *The Fun of It*

Over the Atlantic

Through the afternoon, evening, and following morning, the *Friendship* flew east, through dense clouds and fog, and a few hours of complete darkness. "Not again on the flight [after takeoff] did we see the ocean," said Amelia. Even if they had been able to see the Atlantic Ocean from the air, it would not have helped them navigate—there are no landmarks between Newfoundland and the British Isles.

That meant the trio aboard the *Friendship* had to figure out where in the sky they were using calculations based on time, airspeed, and direction.

They had originally intended to touch down near Southampton, England, but after dumping fuel to ease takeoff, they changed their destination to Valentia, Ireland. This point was about 500 miles (800 km) closer to their point of departure.

"Our Atlantic crossing was literally a voyage in the clouds. Incidentally, the saying about their silver linings is pure fiction. The internals of most clouds are anything but silvery—they are clammy grey [sic] wetness as dismally forbidding as any one [sic] can imagine."

Amelia Earhart, *The Fun of It*

As they neared Ireland, the plan was to contact ships in the area via radio, to confirm their position and to guide them to a suitable landing site. Unfortunately, the plane's radio conked out somewhere over the Atlantic. That meant there was no way to contact ships to figure out where they were—and they couldn't see anything through the fog.

By early afternoon on June 18, the *Friendship* was dangerously low on gas. The aviators still had no way of knowing whether they were following their planned route, or if they had veered off course.

According to their calculations, the *Friendship* should have been approaching the coast of Ireland at this point. Bill dropped the plane below the clouds to take a look. The three crewmates expected to see land. Instead, all they saw was water—meaning they were off course.

"But suddenly out of the fog, on a patch of sea beneath us, appeared a big transatlantic vessel," said Amelia.

They flew circles around the ship, hoping the captain would see them and instruct a sailor to paint the ship's location on the deck. Painting a ship's geographic coordinates (latitude and longitude) was a common practice at the time, to let pilots know exactly where they were on the globe. In this case, though, it didn't happen. Amelia tried dropping a note tied to an orange for weight, but it missed the ship.

Amelia, Bill, and Slim had no idea where they were. One thing they did know was that they were almost out of fuel. Should they land near the ship, knowing they would be rescued? Or should they continue on in hopes of finding land—and accomplishing their mission?

"We knew we had about two hours' gas or a little less than that left, and it seemed sensible to use it up in an effort to complete the job," said Amelia. "So we kept on eastward."

Before long, they spied a few fishing boats that were so small they had to be within miles of a shoreline. Which shoreline it was didn't matter to the three fliers at this point. They just wanted a safe place to set the plane down.

Minutes later, the relieved crew sighted land through the murky fog. They flew the *Friendship* along the shoreline and found a safe landing spot.

After 20 hours and 49 minutes of flying, Amelia, Bill, and Slim set the *Friendship* down near the unidentified coast. They still had no idea where they were, but they didn't care. What mattered was that they were safe, and that Amelia had just become the first woman to cross the Atlantic Ocean by air!

Soaring to Stardom

As it happened, the *Friendship* had landed near the town of Burry Port, Wales, 350 miles (560 km) beyond the crew's intended landing site in Ireland. Once the Burry Port villagers realized they had just become part of aviation history, they gathered by the thousands to celebrate Amelia. Nobody cared about Bill and Slim, even though they were the ones who actually had flown the plane.

The next day, the three aviators flew to Southampton, England, their original destination. Again, Amelia was swarmed by reporters, photographers, and fans. U.S. president Calvin Coolidge sent her a telegram

Crewmates Lou "Slim" Gordon (left of Amelia, holding gear), Amelia Earhart, and Wilmer "Bill" Stultz were given a warm welcome following their landing in Burry Port, Wales, on June 18, 1928—once the townspeople realized what the Friendship, with Amelia aboard, had accomplished!

The Friendship, with Amelia and her two crewmates aboard, is shown leaving Burry Port, Wales, for Southampton, England, their original intended destination.

> *"The arrival of the* Friendship *was the greatest event this remote district [of Wales] has had since the end of the World War when the town's boys came home. Miss Earhart was nearly crushed by the anxiety of the crowd of men, women and children to touch the hem of her flying suit, get her autograph on a slip of paper, wring her hand and congratulate her upon her triumphant passage over the Atlantic."*
>
> *New York Times,* June 18, 1928

congratulating her on her accomplishment: "To the first woman successfully to span the north Atlantic by air, the greatest admiration of myself and the United States."

The next stop for the trio was London, where Amelia spent two weeks being wined and dined, and meeting celebrities from the world of art, entertainment, and politics. She even met future British Prime Minister Winston Churchill.

Finally, at the end of June, the three fliers headed home. They boarded a ship bound for the United States. When they arrived in New York City on July 6, about 5,000 people were on hand to greet them. There was a parade to celebrate their feat, followed by galas, luncheons, and interviews. Three days later, Amelia, Bill, and Slim traveled to Boston, where they drew an estimated 250,000 fans to

This marker, written in English and Welsh, commemorates the landing of Amelia in Burry Port, Wales, as the unintended first stop on her transatlantic flight in 1928.

FLIGHT LOG

In 1930, the people of Burry Port built a monument to commemorate Amelia's transatlantic flight. The obelisk is topped with a weather vane in the shape of the *Friendship*.

> *"I was a passenger on the journey ... just a passenger. Everything that was done to bring us across was done by Wilmer Stultz and Slim Gordon.... I do not believe that women lack the stamina to do a solo trip across the Atlantic, but it would be a matter of learning the arts of flying by instruments only, an art which few men pilots know perfectly now."*
>
> Amelia Earhart, June 1928

parades and events in their honor. Then it was off to Chicago for more celebrations.

Of course, everywhere the aviators went, Amelia got most of the attention. It bothered her that the press and the public largely ignored Bill and Slim, since they were the ones who had done the flying on the transatlantic flight.

One person who wasn't at all bothered by the spotlight on Amelia was publicist George Putnam—in fact, he had arranged it!

George had been involved in the *Friendship* project from the beginning. He was a publisher and promoter who instantly recognized the amount of attention that would be showered upon the first woman to cross the Atlantic by air.

Even though Amelia had done none of the flying on the voyage, George knew she was the one the public would care about. She was the one they would pay money to read about, or to meet, or to hear give a speech. He knew Amelia could be a star.

Admirers turn out to welcome Amelia in London after the final leg of her transatlantic flight in June 1928.

Chapter 5
Queen of the Air

After the initial hubbub over the historic transatlantic flight died down, Bill Stultz and Slim Gordon faded from public view. Thanks to George Putnam's efforts, Amelia Earhart's star continued to shine. For the next year, she toured the United States giving lectures, doing interviews, and promoting everything from lines of luggage to clothing to cigarettes. She also wrote a book about the transatlantic flight called *20 hrs. 40 min.* The book was George's idea. His family-owned publishing company, G. P. Putnam's Sons, published it in the fall of 1928. (To make for a snappier book title, he shortened the flight time by nine minutes.) Single-handedly, George made "Amelia Earhart" a household name.

Amelia poses with a small plane she bought after her transatlantic flight in June 1928. The plane had been flown from Cape Town, South Africa, to London by celebrated Irish aviator Sophie Catherine Theresa Mary Peirce-Evans.

Amelia's Endorsements

After Amelia became a celebrity, companies clamored to have her endorse their products. That meant her name, or her photograph, or a few words from her would appear in advertisements for the items in question. Over the years, Amelia lent her name to such things as luggage, women's clothing, photographic film, cars, motor oil, and cigarettes (even though she didn't smoke). For the product, her endorsement, or support, translated into increased sales. For Amelia, it translated into money to support her flying habit.

Spotlight on Amelia

George made it his business to keep Amelia's name in the news, but he also worked with her to improve her public image. He taught Amelia how to speak clearly into a microphone; he suggested she fly from event to event because it would generate more excitement; and he convinced her to stop wearing hats, so fans could see her famous windblown blond curls.

Amelia went along with all of George's promotional ideas and events, because they brought in the money she needed to continue flying. In the fall of 1928, though, just before her book was published, she took a break from the celebrity circuit to

Publicist George Putnam came up with ways to advance Amelia's career of promoting products as a media celebrity. He convinced her to keep her lips closed when smiling for the camera, as shown in this studio portrait (top left), in order to conceal a gap between her two front teeth, as shown in this unposed photo (bottom left.)

make the coast-to-coast flight she had wanted to do for years. With that, Amelia became the first woman to fly across the United States, coast-to-coast, and back. Upon her return, she took a position as aviation editor at *Cosmopolitan* magazine, a post that gave her a national setting to promote aviation. More specifically, she used her column in *Cosmopolitan* to promote aviation for women.

The next four years were a whirlwind of activity—on the ground and in the air—for Amelia. In the summer of 1929, she bought herself a new plane, a Lockheed Vega. In that aircraft, she participated in the first women-only air race in the United States. It was officially called the Women's Air Derby race—but was more commonly known as the "Powder Puff Derby." Amelia placed third

WOMEN OF THE AIR UNITE

In October 1929, two months after the Powder Puff Derby, a group of participants recognized the need for an organization for female fliers. The organization would offer "a way to get acquainted, to discuss the prospects for women pilots from both a sports and breadwinning point of view, and to tip each other off on what's going on in the industry," stated a letter addressed to the 117 American women who held pilot's licenses at the time.

On November 2, 1929, 26 women met at an airfield on Long Island, New York, to start the process of establishing this association. Two years later, it was ready to launch. By then, 99 pilots had agreed to join the women-only group.

The organization was named the Ninety-Nines, in honor of its charter members. Amelia was elected as its first president.

Today, the Ninety-Nines has thousands of members, with chapters in 35 different countries around the world.

(out of 19 fliers) in the 2,300-mile (3,700-km) race from Santa Monica, California, to Cleveland, Ohio.

Around the same time, she joined the staff of one of the country's first passenger airlines. "My job was to sell flying to women," she wrote, "both by talking about it and by [overseeing] handling passengers." A year later, in 1930, she left that airline and joined another as vice-president. There, she was in charge of public relations and traffic management.

As she continued her whirlwind schedule of public speaking, promoting air travel, judging flying contests, and writing, Amelia also continued setting records in the air. In 1930, she set two women's speed records in her Lockheed Vega. In December of that year, after 15 minutes of training, she became the first woman to pilot an autogiro, an airplane that also had overhead rotors. Four months later, she set an altitude record in the autogiro.

Alone Over the Atlantic

In the early 1930s, pilots all over the world continued the race to set records—for speed, altitude, and distance. Every pilot dreamed of being the first to accomplish the flight over a particular ocean or continent.

For Amelia—and other female fliers— becoming the first woman to *pilot* an aircraft across the Atlantic (rather than being a passenger) remained the biggest prize of all. By the winter of 1932, several women were in the planning stages of such a trip. Amelia and George knew that if any of the others succeeded, it would bump Amelia out of the spotlight.

Airplane or Helicopter?

The autogiro is like an airplane because it has fixed wings and an engine-powered propeller. It also looks like a helicopter, because it has rotors on top. Unlike a helicopter, though, the autogiro's rotors are powered by air passing through them, not by an engine. Think of a pinwheel lying on its side!

Rather than lifting the craft off the ground, the autogiro's rotors give it more lift and stability. That means the aircraft can take off and land on a very short runway.

In 1930, Amelia became the first woman to fly an autogiro. She set an altitude record in one in 1931. She also crashed three different autogiros! After the last crash, in September 1931, Amelia never again flew an autogiro.

An autogiro at a demonstration in France in 1930.

...ARHART"

...met George Putnam, he was married
... After the *Friendship* flight, though,
...s by Amelia's side. As her publicist,
...er to every event, interview, book
...e. He quickly became smitten with
...12 years his junior.
...29, George and his wife divorced. He
...arry him. She said no. Over the next
...again and again. "I was turned down
...he said.
...mber 1930, Amelia agreed to marry
...ven admit to myself that I was in
...ut at last the time came … when
...yself no longer. I couldn't continue
...what I felt for GP was only friendship."
...e married on February 7, 1931.

Amelia *had* to be the first woman to make the dangerous flight. By that time, sadly, seven women had died trying.

Amelia decided she would attempt her solo flight across the Atlantic on the fifth anniversary of Charles Lindbergh's historic transatlantic flight. That gave her just five months to prepare. Like last time, she kept her plans top secret until she was ready to go.

"I received more credit than I felt I deserved [for the 1928 transatlantic flight]. Now I wanted to justify myself to myself. I wanted to prove that I deserved at least a small fraction of the nice things said about me."

Amelia Earhart, explaining why she made the solo flight across the Atlantic

Amelia is shown with Bernt Balchen, an experienced and highly regarded aviator. Amelia hired Bernt in 1931 to help outfit her Lockheed Vega for her 1932 solo transatlantic flight. He pretended he was planning for a trip of his own, in order to keep Amelia's plans secret.

To make sure her Lockheed Vega could make the trip, Amelia had it fitted with a new engine, increased its fuel capacity, and installed the latest instruments and communications devices. Then she practiced with the new equipment "until I felt really confident of my ability to handle the ship, without looking outside the cockpit—that is, flying it solely with instruments."

On the afternoon of May 20, 1932, Amelia flew her Vega from New Jersey to Harbour Grace, Newfoundland. This was to be the starting point for her crossing. (She chose a slightly shorter route than Lindbergh had taken.)

A few hours later, just after 7:00 P.M., on the fifth anniversary of the day Lindbergh had made his historic Atlantic flight, Amelia took to the skies, alone.

The voyage was anything but smooth sailing. Three hours into the flight, a crucial instrument failed, meaning Amelia had no idea how high above the ocean she was. An hour later, she ran into a terrible thunder and lightning storm. Then she noticed a small flame near the engine. Later, ice coated the aircraft, sending it into a spin. She descended to warmer air to melt the ice, but almost touched the waves before she realized how close she was to the ocean.

As dawn broke, fuel in the reserve tank began dripping on Amelia's shoulder. She feared the flame, which still burned, would ignite the fuel—and the whole plane would catch fire.

At this point, she didn't know exactly where she was, but estimated she was south of Ireland. She veered north, hoping to spot land.

Amelia visits with townspeople in Culmore, a section of Londonderry, Northern Ireland. According to reports at the time, the family shown standing in the doorway were among the first people she encountered after her plane touched down in a pasture following her nonstop solo flight across the Atlantic in May 1932.

"I decided that I should come down at the very nearest place, wherever it was."

She ended up landing in a farmer's field in Londonderry, Northern Ireland. "I succeeded in frightening all the cattle in the county, I think."

It turned out that she had initially been on course, and by turning north, took herself about 200 miles (320 km) out of the way. She had

Amelia is shown outside her plane after landing in a field in Northern Ireland following her 1932 transatlantic flight.

traveled so far north that she almost missed Ireland completely!

In spite of all her inflight difficulties, on May 21, 1932, after 14 hours and 56 minutes in the air, Amelia became the first woman—and only the second person ever, after Lindbergh—to fly solo across the Atlantic.

With the flight, Amelia also became the first person to fly the Atlantic twice. She also broke two aviation records in the process—for the fastest Atlantic crossing, and for the longest nonstop flight by a woman.

Amelia wasn't about to stop there, though. Before long, she set her sights on an even greater feat of flight.

A police officer escorts Amelia through a throng of enthusiastic admirers near her landing site in Northern Ireland.

Chapter 6
The Final Flight

After her historic solo transatlantic flight, Amelia continued to set record after record in the sky. In 1932, she became the first woman to fly solo, nonstop, across North America. A year later, she made the same flight again, even faster than the first time. In January 1935, she was the first person to fly solo from Hawaii to California. (Ten pilots had died attempting this flight over the Pacific Ocean before her.) That year, she was also the first-ever pilot to fly solo from Los Angeles to Mexico City, and from Mexico City to New Jersey. She continued to participate in air races and derbies, setting a total of seven women's speed records during her career. Despite all these triumphs, Amelia had her eye on one more prize in the sky.

In Hawaii, just before her record-setting solo flight to California in 1935, Amelia met five-time Olympic medalist Duke Kahanamoku. Duke was not only a championship swimmer. He also helped popularize a sport that few had heard of outside of Hawaii—surfing!

Preparing to Make History

By the end of 1935, Amelia was 38 years old, and she had done pretty much everything she had set out to do as an aviator. By this time, too, commercial air travel had made flight available to the general public—meaning it had lost its mystique, or air of mystery. The public was losing interest in the antics of aviators.

With most of the important flying records broken, and every major flight route across oceans and continents crossed, few "firsts" remained for pilots. For all these reasons, Amelia decided it was time to give up long-distance flying and record setting. Before she hung up her wings, though, there was one more flight she desperately wanted to make—"a circumnavigation of the globe as near its waistline [the equator] as could be."

At this point in aviation history, even a round-the-world flight was nothing new. Five different crews, and one solo pilot, had already circled the globe by the time Amelia set her sights on the voyage.

The difference was that she planned to be the first *woman* to circle

This photo of Amelia was taken in March 1935, shortly after she became the first person to fly solo from Hawaii to California.

Around the World Six Times

Amelia Earhart was not the first person to attempt a round-the-world flight. In fact, had she been successful, her global voyage would have been the seventh such journey.

The U.S. Army Air Service (a forerunner of the U.S. Air Force) was the first group to fly around the world. A team of four planes and eight aviators took off from Seattle, Washington, on April 6, 1924. After 175 days, two of the planes landed in Seattle, completing the flight. The other two planes crashed. Their crews were rescued.

In August 1928, a German pilot set out on the first-ever solo flight around the globe. It took him 15 months to complete the journey. In 1929, another German set the record for the fastest global flight. He did it in a zeppelin, or airship, in 21 days.

In 1931, a pair of pilots—one Australian, the other an American named Wiley Post—beat the zeppelin's speed record. They flew around the world in eight days and 16 hours. Two years later, Wiley did the flight again. This time he flew solo and set a new speed record: seven days and 20 hours. Between Wiley's two flights, a four-man German crew circled the globe in four months.

the globe. In addition, she would set a distance record by taking "the long route," flying as close to the equator as possible. Previous expeditions had traveled farther to the north or south, making for shorter routes.

Amelia and her husband George spent the next year preparing for her adventure of a lifetime.

The first step was to buy a new airplane. Amelia knew her Lockheed Vega was not up to the challenge of a round-the-world trip. The plane she wanted was a modern, twin-engine Lockheed Electra. It was bigger, faster, and more powerful than her Vega. Unfortunately, she and George could not afford to buy one.

Around this time, Purdue University in Indiana came calling for Amelia. The school was a leader in aviation education in the 1930s. It was the first university in the United States to operate its own airport, and it offered flight training to students, for credit. The university's president knew Amelia would fit right in.

He offered her a job as a lecturer and career counselor for young women who wanted to pursue non-traditional, male-dominated career paths. Amelia accepted the position for the 1935–1936 school year.

She wasn't required to spend all her time on campus. Rather, she visited for short blocks of time throughout the year. During one such visit, in November 1935, Amelia attended a dinner party with Purdue faculty, board members, and former students, or alumni. There, she gave a talk about her dream of creating a

Amelia is shown with Dr. Edward C. Elliott, president of Purdue University, examining her newly purchased Lockheed Electra 10E in 1936. Amelia was able to purchase the plane thanks in part to the generosity of many outside donors. Many of those were members of the Purdue community at the time when Amelia was a lecturer at the university.

"flying laboratory" to study the impacts of long-distance flight on pilots. Of course, she needed a new plane—a Lockheed Electra to be exact—to make this dream a reality.

Before the night was out, dinner guests had donated enough money to cover half the cost of the aircraft. Within months, more generous donors came forward, offering up the rest of the cash Amelia needed to buy and outfit the Electra.

The donors had no idea that what Amelia really planned to do with her new aircraft was fly it around the world!

A smiling Amelia Earhart strolls past her new Lockheed Electra 10E.

Around the World— Take One

Amelia's brand new Lockheed Electra 10E was delivered on her 39th birthday, July 24, 1936. It had been built to her specifications, with the global flight in mind. It was an extraordinary craft for its day, one of only two owned at the time.

For the next eight months, mechanics customized the Electra for its mission. They installed extra fuel tanks, specialized navigation equipment, and the most up-to-date communications devices. Meanwhile, Amelia hired a navigator named Harry Manning and planned her round-the-world route.

George managed the business side of the mission. He arranged permission for Amelia to fly through the airspace of every country on her flight path. He organized refueling stops and maintenance checkpoints along the way. He ensured that mechanics and equipment would be waiting at every landing site. "I felt like a master magician and jigsaw puzzle juggler," he said.

The most challenging part of George's job was organizing the crossing of the Pacific Ocean. Amelia intended to land in Hawaii and in New Guinea, just north of Australia—but this was too far to fly without refueling. She needed another port-of-call between these two locations.

At the time, the South Pacific was poorly charted, or mapped. It appeared there was nowhere to stop in this vast stretch of ocean. One day, a government official friend told Amelia about a small piece of uninhabited land located about halfway between Honolulu and New Guinea. It was called Howland Island, and it had just officially become a territory of the United States.

It sounded like the ideal refueling stop for Amelia. Except for one thing. Howland Island didn't have a landing strip.

Friends in High Places

In 1932, Amelia Earhart met President Franklin Roosevelt and First Lady Eleanor Roosevelt. The couple had invited Amelia and her husband George to a private dinner during one of Amelia's lecture tour stops. The two women became instant friends. Eleanor even asked Amelia to give her flying lessons! After the required permit had been arranged, though, the President refused to allow his wife to undertake such a dangerous pastime.

The two women remained good friends for the rest of Amelia's life. Amelia and George stayed at the White House whenever they were in Washington, D.C.

From left to right in this 1933 photo: First Lady Eleanor Roosevelt, Amelia Earhart, Scottish pilots Jim Mollison and his wife, Amy Johnson, and President Franklin Roosevelt.

Fortunately, Amelia had good friends in high places. She got in touch with one of them—U.S. president Franklin Roosevelt—and asked for his help. The president quickly authorized the U.S. Navy to build an airstrip for Amelia on Howland Island.

Even with a new airstrip, the island was a risky choice for a rest stop. From the air, it would be a tiny target in a vast ocean. At just two miles (three km) long and a half mile (800 m) wide, only the most experienced navigator would be able to find Howland Island in the endless Pacific Ocean.

Amelia decided she needed a second navigator for this part of the voyage. She invited Fred Noonan to join her crew. A pilot and sailor with experience in the South Pacific, Fred was also skilled at celestial navigation. That meant he could use the position of the Sun, Moon, and stars to find his way.

At last, with crew in place, aircraft prepared, route planned, and refueling organized, Amelia was ready to go. She was set to launch the expedition she called the "frosting on the cake" of her career.

Late in the afternoon, on March 17, 1937, Amelia's Lockheed Electra took off from Oakland, California, heading west to Honolulu, Hawaii. About 5,000 people were on hand to witness the start of the historic flight. Amelia Earhart and her crew were on their way around the world!

After an uneventful 15 hours and 47 minutes (a new speed record), the Electra touched down in Honolulu. Already, though, it needed servicing. It would be three days before the

Amelia at the controls of her Lockheed 10E Electra, probably just prior to beginning her round-the-world flight in 1937.

plane was repaired and ready to take off on the second leg of the trip: Honolulu to Howland Island.

On March 20, with Amelia at the controls, the Electra sped down the runway—and crashed before takeoff. Amelia, her crew, and witnesses differ on the cause of the accident. Was it a blown tire, or pilot error? A slippery runway, or mechanical failure? The only thing everyone knew for sure was that Amelia's round-the-world flight was over.

The aftermath of Amelia's failed first effort to circumnavigate the globe following a crash prior to take-off on March 20, 1937, in Honolulu. In two months, she would take to the skies again.

An hour after Amelia crashed the Electra in Honolulu, she phoned George. "Her voice weary with sadness, she said she wanted to try again," he said.

Flying into the History Books

True to her word, two months later Amelia was ready to make a second attempt at circling the planet. By then, one of her navigators, Harry Manning, was no longer available. That meant on this trip, it would be just Amelia and the second navigator, Fred Noonan.

This time, too, the pair would fly the Electra in the opposite direction. Because of changes in global wind and weather patterns, they decided to head east from Florida, rather than west from California. The tricky Howland Island landing would now come near the end of the expedition, when pilot and navigator were likely to be exhausted.

In late May, Amelia, Fred, and George flew from Oakland to Miami. So far, they hadn't told anyone Amelia was planning a second attempt at flying around the world. They made the announcement in Miami. There, mechanics spent 10 days inspecting the Electra from nose to tail. They wanted to make sure it was up to the challenge of a 29,000-mile (47,000-km) flight. They made some last-minute repairs to the aircraft and its radio equipment.

On June 1, 1937, in the darkness before dawn, Amelia said goodbye to George. "In the dim chill, we perched briefly on cold concrete steps, her hands in mine," he said. "There is very little one says at such times."

Amelia's Global Travel Companion

Fred Noonan was Amelia's navigator on her round-the-world flight attempt. Born near Chicago in 1893, Fred was an experienced sailor, navigator, and pilot. After a 22-year career at sea, Fred went to work for Pan American Airways. There, he was known as "a navigational genius." He taught navigation and charted air routes over the Pacific Ocean for Pan Am. "If anyone knew the Pacific, Fred did," said one of his coworkers. He was also skilled in celestial navigation, using the Sun, Moon, and stars to find direction.

Fred had a dark side, though. He was a heavy drinker. Amelia knew about this but hired him anyway. She felt she understood him, because her father had also had a drinking problem.

Amelia and her navigator, Fred Noonan, go over a map of the planned route for their attempt to circle the planet in Amelia's Lockheed Electra, which is also shown here.

George watched nervously as Amelia and Fred climbed into the airplane and took off on their historic expedition.

Throughout her journey around the globe, Amelia kept detailed notes about the goings-on of the Electra and its crew.

The *New York Herald-Tribune* was paying her to write articles about the flight for its readers "as it happens, as told by her." In addition, Amelia had a contract with a publisher to write a book about the extraordinary trip. In the book, to be titled *World Flight*, she was to document her thoughts, her experiences, and the challenges she encountered along the way.

"Please don't be concerned. It just seems that I must try this flight. I've weighed it all carefully. With it behind me, life will be fuller and richer. I can be content. Afterward, it will be fun to grow old."

Amelia to George when he asked her not to make the round-the-world flight

To meet these commitments, Amelia sent updates from every stop along her global route. As George wrote in 1937:

"... [H]er narrative of the journey ... came by cable and telephone. Many of those accounts she supplemented with further notes which arrived later by letter. Likewise, she sent back the log-books of the journey, their pages filled with her own penciling, scribbled in the cockpit as she flew over four continents."

Thanks to these updates, Amelia's fans learned that she stopped to do her laundry in Brazil, veered off-course (because of weather conditions) in Senegal, and saw a herd of hippos in Sudan.

Toward the end of the world tour, monsoon rain and wind grounded Amelia and Fred for five days in a place called Bandoeng in the Dutch West Indies (now Bandung, Indonesia). While they were there, Amelia suffered with dysentery, a painful intestinal ailment. The Electra, too, was under the weather. A number of instruments, crucial to safety and navigation, needed repair.

Amelia, at right, stands on the wing of her Lockheed 10E Electra as her navigator, Fred Noonan, enters the cockpit. This photo was taken during a stop in Puerto Rico during their attempt to fly around the world in 1937.

The next stop for the duo was Port Darwin (now Darwin), Australia, where mechanics gave the Electra another nose-to-tail inspection. They repaired the radio direction-finder, which had been malfunctioning throughout the expedition.

On June 29, 1937, Amelia and Fred took off from Port Darwin for the 24th leg of their journey—a 1,000-mile (1,600-km), eight-hour flight to Lae, New Guinea. By the time they landed there, pilot and navigator had flown a total of 22,000 miles (35,400 km) in 28 days.

The aviators were exhausted, but they knew the next two legs of the trip would be their toughest yet. Before departing Lae, Amelia had the Electra serviced once last time, while she and Fred reviewed their flight plans. Amelia phoned in the next installment of her story to the New York newspaper and sent George a telegram.

"My Electra now rests on the edge of the Pacific," Amelia wrote. "Somewhere beyond the horizon lies home and California."

Then, on July 2, 1937, Amelia and Fred took off in the Electra for the 25th—and longest— leg of their global excursion. They departed at exactly 00:00 Greenwich Mean Time. Tiny Howland Island was 2,556 miles (4,114 km) away, a dot of land in the enormous span of the Pacific Ocean.

Dangerous Journey

The Electra left Lae with enough fuel for about 20 hours of flying. Amelia estimated the flight to Howland Island would take about 18 hours, so there was little room for error.

At 07:20 GMT, Amelia reported to radio operators in Lae that she was about 20 miles (32 km) southwest of the Nukumanu Islands. That meant the Electra was traveling slower than expected, and had only covered about one-third of the distance to its destination.

That was the last word anyone heard from Amelia for seven hours. Because she was traveling over the Pacific Ocean, nobody expected to hear from her. She was far out of radio range.

Still, radio operators aboard the U.S. Coast Guard ship *Itasca* waited nervously. They would be the next ones to hear from Amelia. The *Itasca* was stationed at Howland Island with the sole purpose of guiding Amelia in to the tiny landmass.

At 14:18 GMT, *Itasca*'s radio operators picked up their first crackly call from Amelia.

"Cloudy and overcast" was all they heard. They breathed a sigh of relief!

Over the next few hours, the *Itasca* picked up five more calls from Amelia. Repeatedly, the radio operators tried to reply. They were horrified to realize that, while they could hear Amelia, she could not hear them! They would not be able to help her find Howland Island.

The radio operators tried everything they could think of to contact the Electra. They even tried Morse Code. Amelia radioed to say she

Before GPS

Back in the days before satellites, cell phones, and Google maps, navigators relied on radio signals to find their way in difficult situations. On Amelia's round-the-world flight, she used a device called a radio direction finder (RDF) to help her navigate. This was the most up-to-date technology available at the time.

The RDF consisted of a loop-shaped antenna that rotated. As it rotated, it picked up signals sent by other transmitters. When the operator of the RDF located a signal, he or she could calculate the point of origin of that signal.

In Amelia's case, the ship *Itasca*, stationed beside Howland Island, broadcast a signal. The idea was that Amelia would locate *Itasca*'s signal with her RDF, then fly toward it—and to the safety of the Howland Island landing strip.

The RDF only worked, though, if it was on the same radio frequency as the transmitter of the location signal. It is believed that Amelia and the *Itasca* were broadcasting on different frequencies, meaning Amelia's RDF could not pick up the *Itasca*'s signal. Neither she nor her navigator had the training to fully understand how the RDF worked.

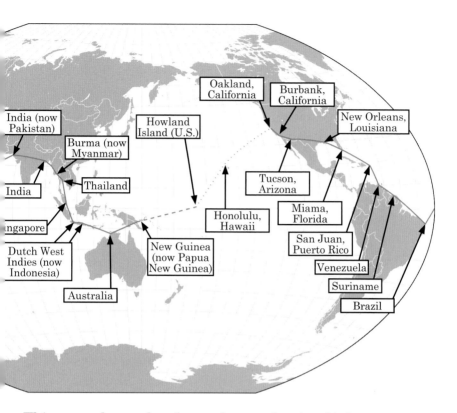

This map shows the planned route for Amelia's round-the-world flight in 1937. The thick lines show the progress of her flight, including key stops or landmarks, until the point, represented by the dashed lines, that the Itasca, *stationed at Howland Island in the Pacific, began having only irregular contact with Amelia. The dotted lines represent the part of the journey that would never be completed. (Note: All locations in U.S. states and territories are identified by name; some of the borders shown on the map reflect the make-up of countries at the time of Amelia's flight.)*

heard it—but neither she nor Fred knew Morse Code, so they couldn't decipher it. Over and over, she asked the ship to give her a directional signal.

Nineteen and a half hours into the flight, the *Itasca* heard this message from Amelia: "We must be on you but cannot see you ... gas is running low." This transmission was so loud, sailors ran outside onto the ship's deck, believing they would see the Electra above them. The sky was clear, but there was no sign of the aircraft.

A few minutes later, Amelia called again: "We are circling but cannot see island. Cannot hear you."

An hour later, at 20:14 GMT, the *Itasca* received one last transmission from Amelia. It gave the position of her aircraft. Then the radio went silent.

Amelia stands with her Lockheed Electra, the plane that she was flying when she lost contact with the U.S. Coast Guard cutter Itasca, *somewhere over the Pacific on July 2, 1937.*

Chapter 7
Loss and Legend

An hour after Amelia Earhart's last contact with the Coast Guard vessel *Itasca*, the ship's captain issued an emergency broadcast to all vessels in radio range. He knew that, by then, Amelia's Electra would be out of fuel and no longer in the sky. He asked other ships to scan the radio waves for signals from her, while the *Itasca* started searching for the downed aircraft. The ship immediately headed northwest to the location Amelia had given in her final call. As the *Itasca* traveled, every available crewmember scanned the ocean and the skies for a sign of the plane— or a sign of life. They saw nothing.

The Search for a Legend

On July 4, 1937, President Franklin Roosevelt authorized a massive search for Amelia, Fred, and the Electra.

About 1,500 members of the U.S. Navy and Coast Guard began to search by air and by sea. At the same time, newspapers around the globe shared the stunning news: "Earhart Plane

Bold yet modest in her demeanor, and well spoken yet unassuming in her manner, Amelia embodied a spirit of style, confidence, and courage that inspired and fascinated millions all over the world.

Lost At Sea"; "Amelia Earhart Missing in the South Pacific"; "Amelia Feared Lost!"

The world was in shock. Amelia's husband George was distraught with disbelief.

Over the next few days, new headlines gave hope: "Radio men hear Earhart's voice"; "Earhart Flares Sighted by Cutter [*Itasca*]"; "New SOS Spurs Hunt for Amelia."

Like most newspapers around the world, the July 5, 1937, edition of the Chicago Herald and Examiner *expressed both the hopes and fears surrounding Amelia's disappearance. The photo in the lower right shows Amelia during a stop in India along her route. Its caption reads: "AMELIA EARHART AT INDIAN AIRPORT. Steps from plane during ill-fated 'round the world hop."*

During this time, a number of professional and amateur radio operators, as far away as Texas and Florida, claimed they heard Amelia and Fred calling for help. The Navy and Coast Guard followed up on the reports, using every bit of information to guide their search.

Most of these radio reports were later found to be hoaxes, but some may have been real. We will never know for sure. Either way, reports of people hearing Amelia's signals stopped within a few days of her disappearance. The "flares" seen by the *Itasca* on July 5 were found to be lightning strikes.

International newspaper headlines reflected this latest disheartening turn of events: "Hopes of Rescuing Lost Fliers Wane"; "Chances Slim for Rescue of World Fliers"; "Naval Airplanes Fail to Locate Amelia Earhart."

After two weeks without any sign of the Electra or the two aviators, President Roosevelt recognized that the hunt for Amelia and Fred was hopeless. On July 18, he called off the search. By this time, the Coast Guard and Navy had scoured 250,000 square miles (650,000 sq km) of the Pacific Ocean looking for the downed fliers. The search cost the U.S. government $4 million, making it the most expensive and thorough search in history to that point.

While the rest of the world may have lost all hope that Amelia would be found alive, George refused to give up on his wife. After the official search ended, he hired private boats to continue looking. Three months later, without finding a single new lead, he too accepted that he would never see Amelia again. George called off his private search in October 1937.

WHATEVER BECAME OF ... ?

- Amelia's husband, George Putnam, remarried two years after Amelia's disappearance. He served as an intelligence officer in World War II, divorcing and remarrying once again soon after the war ended. With his fourth wife, George ran a hotel in Death Valley, California. He died of kidney failure in 1950, at age 62. During his life, George wrote eight books, including *Soaring Wings: A Biography of Amelia Earhart*, in 1939.
- Amelia's mother, Amy, believed her daughter was a spy for the U.S. government and that her disappearance had been faked. Amy stayed in California for years, hoping Amelia would return to California. Eventually, she moved to Massachusetts, where she lived with her other daughter, Muriel. Amy died in 1962 at age 95.
- Amelia's father, Edwin, lived in Los Angeles, California, until his death in 1930 at age 63. By then, he had remarried. He was forever short of money. Amelia helped him out by paying his mortgage, making sure he and his wife always had a home.
- Amelia's sister, Muriel, married and had two children. After her kids grew up, she returned to her teaching career. Unlike her mother, Muriel believed Amelia's plane had crashed into the Pacific Ocean. She kept in touch with George Putnam until his death. Muriel died in Medford, Massachusetts, in 1998 at age 98.

A month later, he published the book Amelia had been writing about her round-the-world voyage. He changed the title of the book, from *World Flight* to *Last Flight*.

At George's request, Amelia Earhart was declared legally dead on January 5, 1939.

After Amelia

In the years following Amelia's disappearance, many theories emerged about what "really" happened to her. The two most likely theories are that her plane ran out of gas and either (a) crashed into the Pacific Ocean, or (b) landed on a nearby, uninhabited island, where Amelia and Fred later died.

Flight Log

It would be 11 years before another woman completed the task Amelia Earhart had set out to do. In August 1949, British pilot Richarda Morrow-Tait became the first woman to fly around the world. She and her navigator completed the journey in one year and one day. They were the first people to complete a global flight after Amelia's failed attempt.

Other, stranger ideas have also been presented.

Some say Amelia became a spy for the U.S. government, and the government sent her into hiding. Others believe Amelia and Fred were captured and killed by the government of Japan—then an enemy of the United States. Another thought is that Amelia was captured by Japan and forced to make anti-American radio broadcasts during World War II. There is no evidence to support any of these ideas.

The oddest theory is that Amelia survived the round-the-world flight, moved to New Jersey, and changed her name to Irene Bolam. This claim was made in a book that was published in 1970. Irene Bolam denied the claim personally and took legal action against the publisher. This resulted in the publisher pulling the book from the marketplace. In more recent years, a state-of-the-art scientific examination based on facial features disproved conclusively the notion of the two women being the same.

In 1988, the International Group for Historic Aircraft Recovery (TIGHAR) launched an investigation into Amelia's disappearance.

Honoring Amelia

In 1967, American pilot Ann Pellegreno successfully made the flight Amelia never finished. On June 9, she took off from Oakland, California, in a Lockheed Electra. She closely followed Amelia's route, arriving back in Oakland on July 7. On July 2, the 30th anniversary of Amelia's disappearance, Ann flew over Howland Island and dropped a wreath in Amelia's honor.

In 1997, on the 60th anniversary of Amelia's failed flight, another American woman, Linda Finch, made the same trip in Amelia's honor. A third, a woman named Amelia Rose Earhart (no relation), completed the same flight in 2014.

Amelia Rose Earhart is shown in the cockpit of her plane in Oakland on June 26, 2014, before departing on a flight retracing the route of her namesake, Amelia Earhart. Amelia Rose hoped that, in addition to providing herself with the adventure of a lifetime and honoring Amelia, the trip would raise awareness about women in aviation.

So far, the organization has funded 11 expeditions to a tiny island called Nikumaroro, south of Howland Island. TIGHAR researchers believe Amelia and Fred landed the Electra near Nikumaroro, at the time called Gardner Island, where they later died.

Over the years, TIGHAR has discovered evidence it believes proves this theory to be true. For example, researchers have found items that could have come from Amelia's or Fred's clothing—a zipper pull, snap, and button. They have found jars and bottles from products Amelia might have used.

TIGHAR's most convincing find was the discovery, in 1991 on Nikumaroro, of a piece of metal. In 2014, after years of study, this scrap of aluminum was "identified to a high degree of certainty" to be a fragment from Amelia's lost Electra.

In addition, during a 2012 TIGHAR mission, sonar imagery showed "an anomaly," something out of place, deep on the ocean floor near Nikumaroro. An expedition in June 2015 to search and photograph the area failed to find evidence when a remotely operated vehicle, or ROV, that was key to the search broke down. The TIGHAR team was able to salvage some images from a less-sophisticated camera system, and as of late 2015 had not announced either the results of analyzing those images or plans for another expedition.

This figure of Amelia Earhart is on display at Madame Tussauds wax museum in Times Square, New York City.

TIGHAR: PRESERVE, EXPLORE, INSPIRE

Founded in 1985, TIGHAR (pronounced "tiger") is The International Group for Historic Aircraft Recovery. The organization is dedicated to finding and preserving rare and "endangered" airplanes of the past. TIGHAR mostly focuses on recovering World War II planes, but since 1988, it has led the search to find Amelia Earhart's Electra.

Since 1985, the group has also been looking for a French aircraft called *l'Oiseau Blanc* ("the White Bird"). This plane and its pilots vanished during an attempted crossing of the Atlantic, just days before Charles Lindbergh made his historic flight.

Star of Stage and Screen

In 2009, actor Hilary Swank starred in a movie about Amelia Earhart's life called *Amelia*. It is at least the fifth film produced about the aviator since her

disappearance. The first, called *Flight for Freedom*, was released in 1943.

Amelia Earhart has also made "appearances" in film and TV projects. For example, Amy Adams played her in *Night at the Museum: Battle of the Smithsonian*. Actor Sharon Lawrence played her in a TV episode of *Star Trek: Voyager*.

Amelia has been the subject of songs, poetry, novels, and children's books. A Canadian theater company presented a musical play about Amelia in 2011. Even Google has honored Amelia, with a Google Doodle on the occasion of her 115th birthday, in 2012.

This photo taken during the shooting of Amelia, *the 2009 bio pic of Amelia's life, shows Hilary Swank in the title role.*

TIGHAR does not buy, sell, or restore the airplanes it finds. Instead, it works with museums and other aviation organizations to make sure the aircraft are treated with "integrity, responsibility, and professionalism."

Despite decades of investigation that has turned up convincing evidence, TIGHAR still

"Amelia's legacy is the legend of an ordinary girl growing into the extraordinary woman who dared to attempt seemingly unattainable goals in a man's world."

Biographer Mary S. Lovell

AMELIA LIVES ON

Decades after her disappearance, Amelia Earhart continues to be honored around the world. Buildings, scholarships, awards, parks, schools, and airports have been named after her. There is a wildlife sanctuary bearing her name in Ireland, near the landing site of her 1932 solo flight across the Atlantic. In 1942, the United States named a World War II cargo ship the *SS Amelia Earhart*. (It was shipwrecked six years later.) In 2008, the U.S. Navy named another cargo ship after the famous flier.

A land formation on the planet Venus is called the Earhart Corona. There is also a minor planet called 3895 Earhart, and a crater on Earth's Moon named Amelia Earhart.

There is an Amelia Earhart Bridge in her hometown of Atchison, Kansas; an Amelia Earhart Dam in Massachusetts; and an Amelia Earhart Regional Park in Miami, Florida.

In 1963, the United States issued a commemorative eight-cent stamp bearing Amelia's photo. Monuments, roads, and statues dedicated to Amelia around the globe will ensure that she is never forgotten.

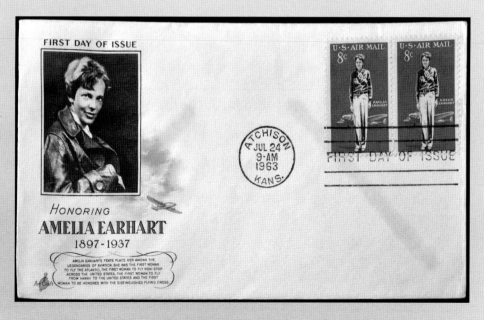

This special "First Day of Issue" cover marks the release of the eight-cent "Amelia Earhart" air mail stamp on July 24, Amelia's birthday. The postmark indicates that the stamp was officially issued in 1963 in Amelia's hometown of Atchison, Kansas.

If you ever fly over Atchison, Kansas, be on the lookout for Amelia's face in a nearby field. In 1997, Stan Herd, a Kansas artist who creates "crop art" and other types of earthworks out of the land, transformed a 42,000-square-foot (3,900-sq-m) parcel of land into a "landscape mural" of the aviator. It is made of grasses, plants, earth, and stone. (Note road at top of photo for size.)

has no absolute proof that the Electra went down near Nikumaroro. Amelia Earhart's disappearance remains one of the greatest unsolved mysteries of the 20th century.

One thing we know for sure about Amelia is that she changed the way society viewed aviation in general, and female aviators in particular.

Amelia lived in a time when women were expected to be wives and mothers—men were the ones to earn money, make decisions, and take risks. Amelia challenged those roles throughout her life. She made it her mission to prove that women could—and should—do whatever they chose to do.

As an aviator, Amelia inspired generations of female fliers who followed in her footsteps. At the same time, her independence, courage, and persistence inspired, and continue to inspire, all sorts of young girls to follow their dreams— whatever those dreams may be.

"Please know that I am quite aware of the hazards. I want to do it because I want to do it. Women must try to do things as men have tried. When they fail, their failure must be but a challenge to others."

Amelia's final letter to her husband

Chronology

July 24, 1897 Amelia Mary Earhart is born in Atchison, Kansas.

1908 Amelia and her family move to Des Moines, Iowa; Amelia sees an airplane for first time.

1912 "Grandmother Otis," the woman who helped raise Amelia, dies.

1913 Amelia and family move to St. Paul, Minnesota.

1914 Amelia and family arrive in Springfield, Missouri, to discover a job promised to her father doesn't exist; Amelia's mother, Amy, leaves her husband, Edwin, and moves to Chicago with her two daughters.

1915 Graduates from Hyde Park High School in Chicago; with her mother and sister, moves to Kansas City, Kansas, to reunite with her father.

1916 Enters the Ogontz School, a "finishing school," in Philadelphia.

1917 Visits her sister Muriel in Toronto, Ontario, Canada.

1918 Quits her studies at Ogontz, moves to Toronto, and becomes a nurse's aide to help soldiers injured in World War I.

1919 Enrolls in pre-med courses at Columbia University in New York City.

1920 At her parents' insistence, quits Columbia and moves to Los Angeles, California, where her now-reunited parents live; takes her first flight in an airplane.

1921 Takes first flying lesson; buys first airplane, a yellow Kinner Airster; names it the *Canary*; becomes a certified pilot through the Aero Club of America.

1923 Becomes 16th woman in the world to earn an international flying license through the Féderation Aéronautique Internationale; sells the *Canary* to raise money to help her family.

1924 Parents divorce; Amelia and her mother take a cross-country road trip, from California to Boston.

1926 Takes job as social worker at Denison House in Boston.

1928 Gets phone call from Captain Hinton H. Railey, asking her if she would like to become first woman to fly across the Atlantic; agrees and becomes first woman to fly (as a passenger) across Atlantic; publishes her first book, *20 hrs. 40 min.*; becomes first woman to fly coast-to-coast, across America and back; becomes aviation editor for *Cosmopolitan* magazine.

1929 Buys a new plane, a Lockheed Vega; places third in the first-ever Women's Air Derby.

1930 Sets two separate air speed records for women; becomes first woman to fly an autogiro.

1931 Amelia marries publisher and publicist George Putnam; sets an altitude record in the autogiro; elected as the first president of the Ninety-Nines, a flying organization for women.

1932 Becomes first woman to fly solo across Atlantic, breaking two aviation records in the process—fastest Atlantic crossing and longest nonstop flight by a woman; is awarded National Geographic Society's Gold Medal, U.S. Army Air Corps's Distinguished Flying Cross, and Cross of Knight of the Legion of Honor from the French government; becomes first woman to fly solo, nonstop, across United States; publishes her second book, *The Fun of It*.

1935 First pilot to fly solo from Hawaii to California; first pilot to fly solo from Los Angeles to Mexico City; first pilot to fly solo from Mexico City to New Jersey; takes a position as lecturer and career counselor at Purdue University in Indiana.

1936 Takes possession of a custom-designed Lockheed Electra 10E.

1937

March 17: Amelia and her crew take off from Oakland, California, beginning her first attempt at a round-the-world flight.

March 20: Plane crashes on takeoff from Honolulu, Hawaii, ending her first round-the-world flight attempt.

June 1: Amelia and her navigator, Fred Noonan, take off from Miami, Florida, to begin their second attempt at a round-the-world flight.

July 2: Amelia and Fred take off from Lae, New Guinea, to fly 25th leg of their global flight; their destination is tiny Howland Island in the Pacific Ocean.

July 2: Makes her final radio call to U.S. Coast Guard cutter *Itasca*; she and Fred and their aircraft vanish over the Pacific.

July 4: President Franklin Roosevelt authorizes what will become the most expensive and intensive search in history; Coast Guard and Navy crews fail to find Amelia, Fred, or their aircraft.

July 18: President Roosevelt calls off search.

November: Amelia's husband George publishes the book she had been writing about her round-the-world flight; title is changed from *World Flight* to *Last Flight*.

January 5, 1939 Amelia Earhart is declared legally dead.

Glossary

alcoholism A disease in which a person is addicted to alcoholic beverages

anomaly An irregularity

antics Silly, funny, or unusual behavior designed to attract attention

ascend To rise above

aviation Related to flying or operating an aircraft

aviator A person who flies or operates an aircraft

barrel roll An aerobatic exercise in which an aircraft flips upside down and rights itself, while flying forward in a corkscrew shape

boarder A person who pays money for a room and meals in another person's home

circumnavigation A flight or voyage that goes completely around the world, or circles the globe

cockpit The part of an airplane where the pilot and/or flight crew sit

coming-out party A formal party in which a girl or young woman is officially introduced to society

cutter A type of ship used for patrol or other official duties

disproportion An unequal or unfair share of something

fixed wings Wings on an airplane that don't move; an aircraft that has such wings is known as a fixed-wing aircraft, as opposed to a helicopter, in which lift and direction are controlled by spinning wings, or blades, called a rotor system

floatplane An airplane that is able to land on water; it floats on pontoons

fly-past A ceremonial flight at a celebration or exhibition; a sort of aerial salute; also called a flyby

forthwith Immediately

Greenwich Mean Time A standard time zone upon which all other time zones are based; it is the time at Greenwich, England, which is located at 0° longitude

hazardous Dangerous, risky

hoax A trick designed to deceive

instigate To start, or set in motion

legally dead A government's certification of a person's death; in absence of a body, this is done after a sufficient period of time has passed, after which the person is presumed dead

log A diary or journal

maneuverable Easy to steer, move, and direct

medieval Relating to the Middle Ages, a period of European history from about A.D. 500 to about 1500

Morse Code A communication system developed in 1836, in which letters of the alphabet are represented by a series of short and long dashes; Morse Code was first transmitted through telegraph wires, and later via radio waves

navigate To plan and direct the route of a ship, aircraft, or other vehicle

obelisk A narrow, four-sided monument that narrows to a point or pyramid at the top

outcast A person who is rejected by a group of people or society

pontoon A watertight floating object, usually a cylinder, that supports a plane, dock, bridge, or other structure

precocious Having developed abilities, behavior, or intelligence beyond one's age; usually describes a child

recuperation Recovery from an illness

rotor A system of rotating wings, as on top of a helicopter

scandalous Shocking, in an offensive way

slip A technique used by pilots to quickly lower a plane's altitude without changing direction or airspeed; during the descent, the plane continues along the same flight path, but it is tilted on an angle

smitten To be strongly attracted to, or in love with, someone

soirée French word, meaning "party"

solo To fly an aircraft alone

spin An aerobatic maneuver in which the aircraft rotates while falling nose-down toward the ground in a corkscrew pattern

stall An aerobatic exercise in which the pilot pulls the nose of the plane upward, slowing to the point at which the wings can no longer support the aircraft; this causes the plane to fall nose-first until speed increases enough for the plane to fly again

stamina The ability to sustain physical or mental strength and energy over a long period of time

supplement To add to or improve something

sympathizer To be on someone's side or to understand how they feel

whim A sudden desire to do something; an impulse

zeppelin A blimp-shaped, gas-filled airship with a metal skeleton to keep its shape

Further Information

Books

Earhart, Amelia. *20 Hrs., 40 Min.: Our Flight in the* Friendship. Washington, DC: National Geographic Society, 2003. (Originally published in 1928.)

—. *The Fun of It*. Chicago: Academy Chicago Publishers, 1977. (Originally published in 1933.)

—. *Last Flight*. New York: Crown Trade, 1996. (Originally published in 1937.)

Video/DVDs

World of Mysteries: In Search of Amelia Earhart (online video). Naked Science, 2002. This full-length video documents Amelia's most famous flights, including her final flight. It presents a different theory about the disappearance than that of TIGHAR. View it for free online at:
https://www.youtube.com/watch?v=KPrBgNXpV7w

Amelia Earhart's Last Photo Shoot (online video). The Paragon Agency, May 1937. This recently discovered film clip shows Amelia, her aircraft, her husband, George, and navigator Fred Noonan in the months before Amelia's round-the-world flight attempt. Available as part of a National Geographic online article called "Newly Discovered Amelia Earhart Film Reignites Mystery":
http://news.nationalgeographic.com/2015/06/150610-amelia-earhart-last-photo-shoot-aviation-discovery0/

Where's Amelia Earhart? (DVD). National Geographic Videos, 2009. This documentary, produced for the National Geographic Channel, uses archival photographs and film footage, as well as reconstructions of historical events, to examine facts and evidence surrounding the last flight and mysterious disappearance of Amelia Earhart.

Amelia (DVD). 20th Century Fox, 2009. Feature-length historical drama about the life of Amelia Earhart, including her doomed attempt to circumnavigate the globe, starring Hilary Swank as Amelia and Richard Gere as her husband, George Putnam.

Amelia Earhart: The Final Flight (DVD). Turner Television Network/Warner Archive Collections, 1994/2013. This made-for-TV film originally appeared in 1994 and starred Diane Keaton as Amelia Earhart, Bruce Dern as her husband, George Putnam, and Rutger Hauer as navigator Fred Noonan. With increased interest in Amelia's life in recent years, the movie was released on DVD in 2013.

Websites

www.ameliaearhart.com/
"Amelia Earhart: The Official Website." This site is a good place to start for photos, news, and information about Amelia. It features a detailed biography, provides many (low-resolution) photos, and lists links to other Amelia-related sites.

http://tighar.org/Projects/Earhart/AEdescr.html
"The Earhart Project." This is not a particularly user-friendly site, but it has everything you could ever want to know about TIGHAR's search for Amelia, Fred, and their aircraft. Click on "The Earhart Project in a Nutshell" to get you started.

**http://airandspace.si.edu/explore-and-learn/topics/
women-in-aviation/**
"Women in Aviation and Space History." This site provides short biographies of 47 different women who have made history as aviators. It includes women of Amelia's generation, along with women who are still flying today.

**http://www.tripline.net/trip/Amelia_Earhart's_Circumnavigation_
Attempt-6410741502631003B225FC83C9742523#photo**
"Amelia Earhart's Circumnavigation Attempt." This page from the interactive-map site Tripline maps out Amelia's final flight, stop-by-stop, with photos and descriptions of many of the locations along the route.

http://interview.sweetsearch.com/2010/10/amelia-earhart.html
"Interview of the Day: Amelia Earhart." This page has links to three fascinating newsreel clips about Amelia's solo transatlantic flight. Two of them are interviews, so you can hear what her voice sounded like.

Index

About the Author

Diane Dakers was born and raised in Toronto, and now makes her home
in Victoria, British Columbia. Diane has been a newspaper, magazine, television,
and radio journalist since 1991. Like Amelia Earhart, she loves to fly. Once,
Diane's pilot brother let her take the controls!